Talking Dollars & Sense

Leading Theological Discussions on Money

Talking Dollars & Sense

Leading Theological Discussions on Money

BRENDAN J. BARNICLE

Church Publishing
19 East 34th Street
New York, NY 10016

Cover design by Jennifer Kopec, 2Pug Design
Typeset by Rose Design

Library of Congress Cataloging-in-Publication Data

Names: Barnicle, Brendan, author.
Title: Talking dollars and sense : leading theological discussions on money / Brendan J. Barnicle.
Description: New York, NY : Church Publishing, [2022] | Includes bibliographical references.
Identifiers: LCCN 2021041817 (print) | LCCN 2021041818 (ebook) | ISBN 9781640654488 (paperback) | ISBN 9781640654495 (epub)
Subjects: LCSH: Wealth--Religious aspects--Christianity. | Money--Religious aspects--Christianity. | Christian leadership. | Church finance. | Christian giving. | Finance, Personal--Religious aspects--Christianity. | Christian stewardship.
Classification: LCC BR115.W4 B37 2022 (print) | LCC BR115.W4 (ebook) | DDC 241/.68--dc23

LC record available at https://lccn.loc.gov/2021041817
LC ebook record available at https://lccn.loc.gov/2021041818

Contents

Introduction

In **the face of declining church attendance** and diminishing religious affiliation in the United States, important conversations are occurring among theologians, clergy, and lay leaders about congregational leadership. As the conversations have developed, however, the importance of financial leadership has not been sufficiently recognized. Over the past four years, I have worked in two very different parish contexts: one parish served a low-income community, while the other served a financially comfortable congregation. Regrettably, in both settings, it was difficult to engage in meaningful theological conversations about money. Some people were embarrassed by how much money they had or did not have. Many became self-conscious once the topic of money was raised. Others depended on the church as a place where they could escape worldly concerns. Yet, in both contexts, a theological conversation about money was essential for congregational development and spiritual growth. What the church needs is an understanding of financial leadership as congregational leadership.

In this book I will argue that congregational leaders, both lay and ordained, can and should provide necessary financial leadership. They can offer the theological and scriptural guidance that is essential for moving this conversation forward. They can introduce tools for assisting economic decision-making at the individual, congregational, and denominational levels. At the same time, they can also help to assuage people's financial anxiety. This book seeks to do four things. First, it discusses field research that attempts to identify the key challenges for congregational leaders in guiding theological conversations about money. Second, it reviews historic theological and scriptural resources. Third, it documents the economic injustice that has been inflicted on people based on their race, gender, and sexual orientation. Fourth, it offers sample curricula, drawing on theological and scriptural resources, that can help leaders guide theological discussions about money. Ultimately, this book strives to demonstrate that, rather than avoiding discussions of money, churches have an active role to play in leading those conversations to reduce financial anxiety and to teach Christian financial leadership. But first you might be asking, "Why does this matter?"

"Why Does This Matter?" Financial Leadership as Congregational Leadership

With so many demands on congregational leaders, it is natural to wonder why they need to take on yet another responsibility. They need to also be financial leaders for several reasons. First, as financial leaders, they can provide transparency into the operations of a church, which can build trust at a time when clergy have historically low ratings for honesty and ethics. Second, financial leadership is critical for maintaining the aging infrastructure of many churches. Third, social scientists confirm that we are living in a time of growing materialism and financial anxiety. Fourth, financial leadership offers not only pastoral support but also prophetic leadership on justice issues. Race, gender, and sexual orientation are significantly associated with wealth disparities in the United States, and financial leaders can help congregations and denominations address the complex issues of justice surrounding money. Finally, as described in chapter 2, Christianity has always provided moral guidance on the use of money, and people need that guidance now more than ever. The church might be the only institution that can provide that direction. While many congregational leaders might prefer to avoid this role, it seems to be a role that God is requiring of them.

Since 1976 Gallup has been conducting surveys and studies regarding the honesty and ethical standards of a variety of professions. Regrettably, ratings for clergy have been steadily dropping. In the 2018 survey only 37 percent of respondents gave clergy a "very high/high" rating, which is the lowest percentage for clergy in the history of the survey. The overall average positive rating was 54 percent, well below the historical high of 67 percent. Views of clergy were particularly damaged by the sexual abuse scandals in the Roman Catholic Church in the early 2000s, and clergy ratings have never fully recovered. While positive ratings have rebounded somewhat, they fell to 50 percent in 2009 and have been steadily declining since 2012.[1]

During the focus group research conducted for this book, it became clear that members of the groups had concerns about the lack of transparency in spending by religious congregations. Many people had been members of congregations where they did not know how money was spent. While most respondents did not assume ill intent, they expressed skepticism because leaders did not provide consistent financial information. In most cases, respondents acknowledged that leaders lacked the requisite financial expertise to provide transparency. Nevertheless, respondents have come to expect a certain level of transparency from other institutions, and they also expect it from their churches. Coupling a lack of transparency with a drop in expectations of honesty and ethical behavior from clergy is a recipe for distrust. The best way for church leaders to respond to these concerns is to improve financial transparency, particularly

1. Megan Brenan, "Nurses Again Outpace Other Professions for Honesty, Ethics," Gallup, December 20, 2008, accessed September 7, 2020, *https://news.gallup.com/poll/245597/nurses-again-outpace-professions-honesty-ethics.aspx?utm_source=alert&utm_medium=email&utm_content=morelink&utm_campaign=syndication.*

with the church's annual budget and its quarterly financial results. These two financial markers demonstrate the church's values and offer an example of the role that money plays in Christian discipleship. In fact, Archbishop of Canterbury Justin Welby has suggested that church budgets are excellent examples of practical theology; they demonstrate how theology is applied in the world.[2]

Another significant challenge facing the church is aging infrastructure. After World War II, the United States experienced an economic boom that benefited most major Christian denominations. More church buildings were constructed during the postwar period than in any comparable period of US history.[3] Now, seventy-five years later, many congregations are confronted with aging buildings, outdated plumbing, insufficient wiring, and inadequate information technology to support their current needs. Remodeling or selling these buildings requires extensive legal and financial work. While congregations will hire lawyers and work with financial advisors, church leaders need to provide financial leadership to steward these resources. Otherwise, they risk losing these great assets and undermining the church's missional work. In many cases, the rector is the only hired professional at a church, and the congregation will expect him or her to look after the property along with the souls of the congregation. Yet, leaders need specific skills to exercise their proper fiduciary and canonical duties. When the church and its leaders are wary of confronting financial matters, they lose their ability to demonstrate how to manage money and wealth in ways that are consistent with the gospel. With its assets, the Episcopal Church could be a model for Christian money management and stewardship. It is a model that the world desperately needs.

2. Justin Welby, *Dethroning Mammon: Making Money Serve Grace* (London: Bloomsbury, 2016), 126.

3. Mark A. Noll, *The Old Religion in a New World: The History of North American Christianity* (Grand Rapids, MI: Eerdmans, 2002), 159.

Since the 1960s, social scientists have observed an increase in materialism around the world.[4] In 1961 philosopher René Girard introduced the theory of the "memetic nature of desire" in his first book, *Deceit, Desire, and the Novel.*[5] His theory posits that humans desire the things that they see that others have. In an increasingly connected and global context, memetic desire can extend to virtually everyone and everything. Therefore, people feel even greater pressure to keep up with their proverbial neighbors. Colloquially, this might also be called "the fear of missing out." Biblically, it is known as covetousness. This fear is driving materialism, and materialism is driving financial anxiety. In addition, the economic downturn of 2019–20 has exacerbated financial anxiety. In response, consumers turn to the market for help: more shopping, more prescription drugs, more alcohol, more distractions and amusements. In so doing, most people largely ignore the underlying fear. If congregational leaders could step into this landscape of uncertainty and fear and offer pastoral care, they could truly continue in the healing work of Jesus. To provide such relief, congregational leaders need to offer financial leadership. They need confidence in their own personal financial budgets and spending. They need to model how a Christian might spend money, and then they need to lead their congregations in theological discussions of materialism, financial anxiety, and money.

Financial anxiety is not the only issue that can be addressed with a theological discussion of money; congregational leaders can also address economic injustice in the world. In fact, financial anxiety and economic injustice are often interrelated. Generally, people

4. Russell A. Belk, "Three Scales to Measure Constructs Related to Materialism: Reliability, Validity and Relationship to Measures of Happiness," *Advances in Consumer Research* 11 (1984): 291–97, accessed September 17, 2021, *https://www.acrwebsite.org/volumes/6260/vol.*

5. Rene Girard, *Deceit, Desire, and the Novel*, trans. Yvonne Frecerro (Baltimore: Johns Hopkins University Press, 1965), 24.

with the fewest resources experience the greatest financial anxiety. Yet wealthy individuals experience financial anxiety too. Global capitalism fuels financial anxiety; in fact, it requires anxiety to propel its growth. From mounting consumer debt to targeted internet advertising, the global economy encourages people to buy more things, which drives up their financial anxiety for a variety of reasons including envy and debt. Finally, some find themselves living in dire poverty. In 2019, 10.5 percent of the US population lived below the national poverty level, according to the United States Census Bureau.[6] According to the World Bank, global poverty was expected to rise in 2020 for the first time in a generation. Roughly seven hundred million people were projected to be living on less than two dollars per day by the end of 2020.[7] Dismantling financial anxiety may start with pastoral care, but it can only end with a more just and equitable economy. The Baptismal Covenant calls for justice and peace among all people. Financial anxiety, particularly among the poor, is the result of injustice and disrupts God's peace. Therefore, Christians are required to act.

Finally, a theological discussion of money is deeply embedded in the Abrahamic traditions. It is rooted in Judaism, and it continues in Islam. It is entirely appropriate for contemporary Christian leaders to continue this discussion. To be financial leaders, congregational leaders will certainly need training in contemporary finances, budgeting, and accounting, but the theological resources are centuries old. Chapter 2 provides an overview of those resources. Chapter 3 reviews the history of stewardship in the church. Chapter 4 discusses

---

6. Jessica Semega, Melissa Kollar, Emily A. Shrider, and John Creamer, "Income and Poverty in the United States: 2019," United States Census Bureau, Report Number P60-270, September 15, 2020, accessed September 17, 2021, *https://www.census.gov/content/dam/Census/library/publications/2020/demo/p60-270.pdf.*

7. The World Bank, "Poverty: Overview," October 7, 2020, accessed November 18, 2020, *https://www.worldbank.org/en/topic/poverty/overview.*

some of the most commonly cited biblical passages relating to money. Chapter 5 includes background information necessary for leading theological conversations of money that consider the racial, gender, and sexual identity injustices of global capitalism. Chapters 6, 7, and 8 provide sample curricula to lead these conversations. They are linked to Years, A, B, and C of the liturgical calendar, and they focus on personal discipleship, congregational ministry, and global mission, respectively. While this work will require training, time, and patience, it is part of the call to build God's Beloved Community.

CHAPTER

1

"What Are We Afraid Of?"

Financial Anxiety Inside and Outside of Church

Generally, people are anxious about money because they fear that they do not have enough. Without adequate money, they worry about their safety and well-being. A recent study from PNC Advisors found that even wealthy people share this fear. Most people believe that in order to feel secure, they need to double their current net worth, regardless of their financial status.[1] The research surveys conducted for this book confirmed these findings. In fact, in some of the surveys, people with the lowest incomes reported less financial anxiety than those with midlevel incomes. Typically, however, financial anxiety is inversely related to income. The higher your income, the less likely it is that you will experience anxiety. Notably, some affluent people are embarrassed by their wealth or the ways in which they earned it, and they are equally uncomfortable talking about their financial concerns. It seems that no one can escape financial anxiety. Yet, no one wants to talk about it, which only feeds the anxiety.

1. Jim Wallis, *Rediscovering Values: A Guide for Economic and Moral Recovery* (New York: Howard Books, 2011), 110.

From the surveys and focus groups completed for this book, respondents reported both financial anxiety and a strong Christian faith; relatively few, however, had any interest in theological discussions of money. When people hear about money in church, many automatically assume that the church is asking for money, and they tune out altogether. Other people find open discussions of money and church completely irreconcilable. They come to church to elevate their souls, and they presume talk of money will do the exact opposite for them. Survey respondents claimed little interest in classes on theology and money or discussions of money during worship, yet they were open to innovative ways of talking about money in church. A survey of clergy found similar results. For example, they expressed considerable interest in applying the concept of the Trinity to personal finances. If we refer to the Trinity as Creator, Redeemer, and Sustainer, rather than as Father, Son, and Holy Spirit, what might it mean to spend our money in ways that are creative, redemptive, and sustaining? If the Trinity is a community of three persons, what would it mean to spend our money in ways that are cooperative, communal, and anticompetitive, as suggested by the social Trinity? Could a Trinitarian approach to money reduce our financial anxiety? Or would it merely shift the focus? Could it help create a more just and equitable economy? These questions intrigued people in the focus groups, and they are the types of questions that can drive a theological discussion of money.

This chapter considers the myriad reasons for financial anxiety. Theologically, financial anxiety has roots in materialism, idolatry, mimetic desire (i.e., the desire to have what others have), envy and rivalry, and individualism. These themes run throughout scripture and Christian theology. Recalling the ways in which the church has discussed these topics in the past should help us understand how to cope with our own financial anxiety and how to care for others who experience it.

Materialism

Since the 1960s, social scientists have observed a dramatic increase in materialism around the world. Materialism is defined as "a preoccupation with or stress upon material rather than intellectual or spiritual things."[2] Several factors are fueling the growth of global materialism, but perhaps the most significant is the need of individuals for identity and a sense of self. Material objects can help us define ourselves, and advertisers have reinforced the power of their brands to serve this end. Products have become aspirational. At some level, advertisers have convinced us that their products will make us happier and healthier. Consequently, in challenging times, people are increasingly turning to material things to define themselves. In their 1981 book *The Meaning of Things: Domestic Symbols and the Self*, sociologists Mihaly Csikszentmihalyi and Eugene Rochberg-Halton concluded that "things embody goals, make skills manifest and shape the identities of their users."[3]

Material possessions are not inherently bad. In fact, they can enhance individual spirituality and congregational worship. However, material things become a problem when people become too dependent on them to define their lives. Ultimately, objects and possessions fail to satisfy human desires, and they lead to greater anxiety and the unquenchable desire for more. As a result, materialism frequently drives both envy and rivalry. Therefore, Csikszentmihalyi and Rochberg-Halton advocate striking a balance between our need for material objects and the way in which those objects build self-perception. Sadly, humans have not heeded their advice.

---

2. Merriam-Webster Dictionary, s.v. "materialism," accessed September 29, 2020, *https://www.merriam-webster.com/dictionary/materialism.*

3. Mihaly Csikszentmihalyi and Eugene Rochberg-Halton, *The Meaning of Things: Domestic Symbols and the Self* (Cambridge: Cambridge University Press, 1981), 1.

Long before Csikszentmihalyi and Rochberg-Halton, Jesus and many Christian theologians warned about the risks of materialism and argued for simple lifestyles. The patristic fathers; Thomas Aquinas; twentieth-century Msgr. John Ryan, S.J.; and, most recently, Bishop Julio Murray of Panama have all been proponents for a "virtue of sufficiency." A virtue of sufficiency compels people to keep only the money they need to support themselves and to share the rest with others. This virtue presupposes that God's abundance is sufficient to take care of everyone as long as people are willing to share. However, the virtue of sufficiency runs into a challenge when it comes to the specifics of determining what is sufficient. What is sufficient for one person might not be sufficient for another. In the past, various religious leaders have tried to establish guidelines for sufficiency. Today, some people are continuing this effort. One recent example is the Plentitude Movement, which encourages people to embrace a world of abundance rather than scarcity.[4] Communities within the Plentitude Movement share their resources and barter their goods and services. The Plentitude Movement is new, but similar movements follow a long tradition of intentional communities that value simplicity. From St. Benedict's Rule of Life to St. Francis's embrace of poverty, from Amos Bronson Alcott's transcendentalist commune to the Catholic Worker communities, all have tried to offer an alternative economic lifestyle and a new understanding of sufficiency. Members of Christian communities have consistently sought ways to embrace simplicity and overcome materialism. Yet, despite these valiant efforts, materialism continues to gain strength around the world.

Materialism has two direct impacts on financial anxiety. First, it creates anxiety because people are misled to believe that they do not have enough. They are seduced by the false belief that they need

---

4. Juliet B. Schor, *Plentitude: The New Economics of True Wealth* (New York: Penguin Press, 2010), 4–7.

more things to fully define themselves. This anxiety can manifest as hoarding at one extreme and excessive frugality at the other. People want others to acknowledge and appreciate them, and they believe that possessions will help them achieve this goal. People also want to possess more than their peers. In fact, studies show that people care more about their relative economic position than their absolute position.[5] Finally, people are deathly afraid of downward mobility.[6] Downward mobility is anathema to the American dream, and most will go to tremendous lengths to limit their losses. Therefore, materialism inevitably puts people in conflict with each other, creating envy and rivalry as individuals try to outdo each other.

Materialism also creates financial anxiety because people buy things they cannot afford. As a result, they rack up enormous consumer debt, which creates ongoing anxiety in the struggle to pay off those debts. Debt has the potential to reduce human beings, who are equal in God's eyes, into a dominant creditor and a subordinate debtor. The Israelites understood the disorienting impact of debt and sought to manage it with prohibitions against usury, the Jubilee's cancellation of debts, and the Sabbath.[7] Psalm 37:21 even suggests that it is virtuous to forgive debts and a blessing to have one's debt forgiven: "The wicked borrow, and do not pay back, but the righteous are generous and keep giving" (Ps 37:21). While it may sound like a chastisement of debtors, it really only criticizes those who do not repay their own debts and forgive debts owed to them. The Israelites also realized that money was meant to circulate through the economy. When one individual accumulated a lot of money, this capital was not put to work in the economy. Conversely,

5. Robert Skidelsky and Edward Skidelsky, *How Much Is Enough: Money and the Good Life* (New York: Other Press, 2012), 149.

6. Gawain de Leeuw, *The Body of Christ in a Market Economy: An Anglican Inquiry into Economic Thinking* (New York: Peter Lang, 2019), 78–79.

7. de Leeuw, *Body of Christ*, 12–14.

as money changed hands, more people benefited from it. Therefore, the Israelites rightly feared that accumulated wealth and debt would disrupt the economy's proper functioning.

The various causes of financial anxiety are discussed in much of the current secular writing on the topic. There are several practical personal financial solutions: creating budgets, following one's credit score, and working with a financial advisor. These are all sound practical steps, but they do not address the underlying causes of materialism and financial anxiety: idolatry, mimetic desire, envy and rivalry, and individualism. Fortunately, a theological discussion of money can shed light on these issues.

Idolatry

Following the Exodus from Egypt, the Israelites focused on the second commandment against idolatry: "You shall not make for yourself an idol, whether in the form of anything that is in heaven above, or that is on the earth beneath, or that is in the water under the earth. You shall not bow down to them or worship them" (Exod. 20:4–5). Yet, Israel still succumbed to idolatry, and the Israelites created the Golden Calf at the base of Mount Sinai (Exod. 32:4). They understood how tempting it can be to have a concrete idol that serves as a stand-in for an invisible God. Numerous things can become idols in our lives, but money is one of the most popular and seductive. It can fund armies, industries, and space exploration. It can have enormous impact on politics and culture.

The writers of Deuteronomy understood the link between idolatry and desire. In Deuteronomy 7:25, when describing the divine covenant, Moses declared, "The images of their gods you shall burn with fire. Do not covet the silver or the gold that is on them and take it for yourself, because you could be ensnared by it; for it is abhorrent to the Lord your God." Biblical scholar Walter Brueggemann points out that this language reveals a deep concern that coveting is dangerous because that which we covet frequently becomes an idol for us, drawing us away from God and from each other.[8]

Mimetic Desire

In an increasingly connected and global context, memetic desire can extend to virtually everyone and everything. Global capitalism seeks to reinforce perceived needs and desires as a way to drive ongoing sales. If people do not already feel that they need what others have, advertising has encouraged their desire and validated it. Subsequently, people feel even greater pressure to acquire the things that other people have. Internet platforms have accelerated mimetic desire, and they understand our desires better than we understand them ourselves. Moreover, the algorithms that run these platforms know how to manipulate our desires. The internet is largely designed to entice us into spending more time online so that advertisers can sell more things to us. In addition, as we spend time online, internet platforms learn about us, which enhances their ability to exploit us and our desires. The business models behind these platforms are designed to convert our wants into needs, which drives greater financial anxiety.

In biblical terms, mimetic desire is known as covetousness. The Israelites also focused on the tenth commandment against coveting: "You shall not covet your neighbor's house; you shall not covet your neighbor's wife, or male or female slave, or ox, or donkey, or anything that belongs to your neighbor" (Exod. 20:17). The Israelites understood that desire fuels coveting and that coveting can be incredibly powerful, seductive, and disruptive. Israel had experienced it. The book of Genesis documents Pharaoh's endless coveting and its tragic consequences for Israel. When the Israelites were enslaved in Egypt, they were forced to work endlessly to satiate

8. Walter Brueggemann, *Money and Possessions* (Louisville, KY: Westminster John Knox Press, 2016), 39.

Pharaoh's unrelenting fear about not having enough grain to sustain himself and his court. In a different context, the sons of Jacob abandoned their brother Joseph to slavery because they coveted their father's attention. Coveting is not only about desiring what belongs to another; it also includes seizing what belongs to another.[9]

Arguably, the threat from covetousness is even greater today than it was for the Israelites. Covetousness is rarely viewed as a sin in modern culture—in fact, it might even be framed positively as ambition or enthusiasm—yet it has dire consequences. The sin of coveting can lead to other sins, including stealing (sixth commandment), adultery (seventh commandment), and bearing false witness (eighth commandment). In fact, Brueggemann argues that covetousness ultimately leads to idolatry (second commandment), rather than the other way around.[10] René Girard concluded that social prohibitions, like the Ten Commandments, are attempts to control mimetic desire.[11] The people who developed these prohibitions were acutely aware of its destructive power.

Envy and Rivalry

Envy and rivalry can quickly emerge from mimetic desire. Humans are constantly comparing themselves to others; we build our identities in this way. When we cannot get what others have, we become envious, and bitter rivalries can develop. The Episcopal priest and scholar the Rev. Dr. Gawain de Leeuw points out that envy reflects a fear of loss, and it increases our dissatisfaction with the world and increases the anxiety in our lives.[12] If envy

9. Brueggemann, *Money and Possessions*, 38.

10. John Durham, *Word Biblical Commentary: Exodus* (Grand Rapids, MI: Zondervan, 1987), 298.

11. Girard, *Deceit, Desire, and the Novel*, 16.

12. de Leeuw, *Body of Christ*, 26–27.

is not controlled, it can grow into rivalry, which can seed hate, contempt, and even violence. Throughout the Old Testament are stark reminders of the destructive power of rivalry: Cain and Abel (Gen. 4:1–16), Sarah and Hager (Gen. 16), David and Uriah (2 Sam. 11–12), Jacob and Esau (Gen. 25:19–34), and Ahab and Naboth (1 Kings 21:1–15).[13] Again and again, scripture demonstrates the disastrous effects of rivalry. It tears apart the body of Christ and destroys God's creations.

In response to rivalry, people resort to all sorts of behaviors that are contrary to the gospel. There can be violence, as witnessed in the Old Testament; there can also be theft, adultery, and bearing false witness. A more contemporary response is the rise of consumerism. To avoid feeling inferior, people buy the products they believe will make them look like they are doing better than others in hopes that others will envy them.[14] This perverse logic tears at the body of Christ and divides it, undermining the gospel.

Jesus demonstrated how we can transcend rivalry. He redirected his disciples away from rivalry toward a radically new notion of a good life, one that included a Sabbath, rest, and joy. He also taught practices to his disciples that would help them alleviate rivalry: praying in private rather than in public, taking the lowest seat rather than the best seat at the table, and rejecting status of all kinds.[15] He encouraged his disciples to avoid public attention so that they would not attract the envy of others and end up in rivalries. When the mother of James and John asked Jesus to give her sons preferential treatment, Jesus politely asked if they were willing to suffer as he would suffer (Matt. 20:20–28). When Jesus overheard the disciples bickering over who was the greatest among them, he said, "All who exalt themselves will be humbled, and all who humble themselves

---

13. de Leeuw, *Body of Christ*, 26.

14. de Leeuw, *Body of Christ*, 136.

15. de Leeuw, *Body of Christ*, 129.

will be exalted" (Matt. 23:12). In the same situation in Luke's gospel, Jesus made the radical claim that "the least among all of you is the greatest" (Luke 9:48).

As the embodiment of divine humility, Jesus is the ultimate antirival, and he provided a model for how individuals, congregations, and denominations can move beyond envy and rivalry. Jesus's ministry demonstrated anticompetitive ways to live that transcend mimetic desire, envy, and rivalry. He demonstrated this practice when he graciously accepted the anointing of his feet by a woman who came to visit him (Matt. 26:7; Mark 14:3–7; Luke 7:36–50; John 12:1–8). The disciples complained about the expense of the ointment and the background of the woman. When Jesus saw their envy and rivalry, he expressed his appreciation for her love, and he assured his disciples that she had been redeemed. Jesus's world is not one of accounting for every penny but one that is transfixed on love. His vision moves beyond the desires and envy of this world. Similarly, when he was confronted with the adulterous women, he did not rush to judge her. Jesus demonstrated a love that is not competitive, not envious, and not rivalrous.

In addition, Jesus was also clear that he did not seek to destroy rivalry, for in so doing, he would have destroyed a dimension of human beings that God created. Instead, Jesus called on us to redirect the desires that God has created in the world, turning them away from rivalry and scapegoating and back toward God. The family systems theory therapist and Jewish rabbi Edwin Friedman would call this the "non-anxious presence," the person who can confront, but not exacerbate, the surrounding anxiety.[16] Jesus plays this role again and again in the Gospels. When confronted by the Pharisees, the Sadducees, the Herodians, the Samaritans, and even

16. Edwin H. Friedman, *A Failure of Nerve*, 10th anniversary rev. ed., ed. Margaret M. Treadwell and Edward W. Beal (New York: Church Publishing, 2017), 16.

Satan, Jesus did not become anxious. He did not worry about rivals; instead, he turned his focus back to God and back to love. It is challenging, of course, for everyone to live out the gospel.

Rivalries are not limited to individuals. Often, they develop between congregations and denominations that compare themselves to each other and experience the same underlying mimetic desire that affects individuals. Unfortunately, church bodies may be even less equipped to discuss it than individuals. Any discussion of money in an Episcopal church is likely to lead to comparisons with other churches and complaints about the diocese. Nevertheless, these conversations offer an opportunity to explore the emotions that are driving these comparisons. In some ways, it might be safer for people to discuss these topics in the context of a congregation rather than in the context of their own lives. Rejecting rivalry can also have profound economic consequences that help free people from financial anxiety. When people refrain from competitive consumption, they can be liberated from possessions, and they can start to connect in deep, meaningful ways with each other. They might also reduce their personal debt and control their spending. As theologian Eve Poole observes, "Desire is part of the human condition, and our spiritual task is not to resist it, but to curve it away from materialism back towards God."[17] Having open conversations about desire and rivalry lays the groundwork for strong theological discussions of money and for dismantling financial anxiety.

Individualism

Finally, individualism also compounds financial anxiety. A 2017 study published in *Psychological Science* found that individualism is increasing around the world and has increased globally by

17. Eve Poole, *Buying God: Consumerism and Theology* (New York: Church Publishing, 2019), 99.

12 percent since 1960.[18] Individualism is also directly correlated to economic development. As an economy strengthens and grows, individualism grows along with it.[19] In a culture that believes that everyone is supposed to look exclusively after themselves, there is little urgency in the mission of helping others. When people are not confident that they can turn to others for help, their anxiety naturally increases, particularly their financial anxiety.

In the United States, individualism has arguably become an idol. American individualism is rooted in New England Puritanism and in Jeffersonianism; it is reflected in both the Declaration of Independence and the United States Constitution. Individualism and personal freedom have always been important to the development of the culture, politics, and economy of the United States. In the nineteenth century, Romanticism and individualism became the predominant schools of thought in the United States and Europe. In fact, Girard asserts that in the twentieth century researchers and philosophers became afraid to challenge individualism because of the "political and social imperatives of their community."[20]

Despite its popularity in academic, economic, and political circles, individualism is not endorsed by scripture. In fact, the gospel attempts to move followers of Christ beyond an individualistic interpretation of scripture to a communal focus.[21] Rather than focusing narrowly on individual salvation, scripture describes

---

18. "Individualistic Practices and Values Increasing Around the World," Association of Psychological Science, July 17, 2017, accessed October 10, 2020, *https://www.psychologicalscience.org/news/releases/individualistic-practices-and-values-increasing-around-the-world.html.*

19. Henri C. Santos, Michael E. W. Varnum, and Igor Grossman, "Global Increases in Individualism," in *Psychological Science* 28, no. 9 (2017): 1228–39.

20. René Girard, *Things Hidden Since the Foundation of the World*, trans. Stephen Bann and Michael Metteer (Stanford, CA: Stanford University Press, 1978), 7.

21. Brueggemann, *Money and Possessions*, 15.

a "new heaven and a new earth" that includes all of God's creation (Isa. 65:17; Rev. 21:1). The same communal vision applies to money and possessions. Paul reiterated a belief in a communal economy in 2 Corinthians 8:1–15. He commended the community in Macedonia for its support of other communities, despite their own poverty. Giving from their poverty reflected Christ's "law of neighborliness."[22]

In covenantal Judaism, all possessions were believed to have come from God; therefore, they needed to be shared among all of God's people. In fact, Judaism viewed individualism as a risk. If someone had too much autonomy, that person might lose sight of God. Warnings against self-sufficiency appear in Deuteronomy and Psalms.[23] "Do not say to yourself, 'My power and the might of my own hand have gotten me this wealth'" (Deut. 8:17). "In the pride of their countenance the wicked say, 'God will not seek it out'; all their thoughts are, 'There is no God'" (Ps. 10:4). "They think in their heart, 'We shall not be moved; throughout all generations we shall not meet adversity'" (Ps. 10:6).

Ironically, despite the fixation on individualism in the United States, individualism may be a kind of delusion. We are all entirely dependent on one another. In fact, some metaphysical and epistemological hypotheses suggest that our minds are not truly independent and that "our choices are merely perceptions in a highly determined universe."[24] Rev. Dr. de Leeuw challenges notions of individuality and suggests the existence of "interindividuality."

In mimetic theory, human consciousness is therefore interindividual. While a person might perceive being individuated, or separate from other people, their consciousness cannot be neatly disentangled from the outside influences of other people. Desires are not invented

---

22. Brueggemann, *Money and Possessions*, 237.

23. Brueggemann, *Money and Possessions*, 120.

24. de Leeuw, *Body of Christ*, 75.

internally from a blank slate, but learned. A person's tastes and a worldview arise out of family, community, and culture.[25]

From this perspective, instead of actual individuality, there is an illusion of separateness. If people believe that they are individuals, they are expected to demonstrate their individuality, and that largely occurs through possessions such as cars and clothes. However, an excessive focus on individuality risks envy, rivalry, and, ultimately, a loss of care and compassion for others. It can result in egotism and a lonely life that becomes consumed with the next acquisition and that loses sight of God and God's people.

In contrast, Jesus offers a life of community, in which we are all part of the same body of Christ. While we might have different roles in the body and we might not fully appreciate other parts of the body, we are still part of a single body of Christ. The church offers opportunities for people to enter into community, and it does so in a way that is essentially equal for all. Like Jesus, the church can serve as an antirival that enables people to move beyond individuality and its resulting anxiety into becoming God's Blessed Community and sharing God's abundant love.

Money Systems

The surveys conducted for this book reveal the challenge of leading a theological discussion of money; money can be an emotional trigger for people and for organizations. Bowen family systems theory maintains that conflicts over money in families or congregations are never really about the money but reflect a deeper anxiety in the family or the congregation.[26] Therefore, if approached properly, money

---

25. de Leeuw, *Body of Christ*, 126.

26. Margaret J. Marcuson, *Money and Your Ministry* (Portland, OR: Marcuson Leadership Circle, 2014), 18; Friedman, *A Failure of Nerve*, 67; Peter L. Steinke, *Congregational Leadership in Anxious Times* (Lanham, MD: Rowman & Littlefield, 2006), 14–15.

can actually open up a conversation about challenges in a system. For example, conflicts and conversations about money can reveal who is overfunctioning and who is underfunctioning in a system. Overall, financial conflicts that arise offer a critical lens for congregational leaders to better understand themselves and their congregations and, ultimately, to provide necessary leadership. Therefore, discussions about money can be a uniquely powerful way to access the health of a congregation and to discern the pastoral and formational needs of its members. While no one enjoys difficult financial situations, financial leadership can help systems improve.

The pastoral programs presented in chapters 6, 7, and 8 offer resources to initiate theological discussions about money. The programs include congregational forums and exercises. These exercises are pedagogical tools designed to help people discern how God is calling them to view money, possessions, and financial anxiety. Even with resources, this will not be easy work, and leaders will need to reiterate the importance of this work to their congregations.[27] Despite the challenges involved, financial leadership is critical because it can help individuals, congregations, and denominations reduce anxiety, grow in faith, and more fully become God's Beloved Community.

27. Ronald Heifetz and Marty Linsky, *Leadership on the Line: Staying Alive Through the Dangers of Change* (Boston: Harvard Business Review Press, 2017), 55, 75, 141.

CHAPTER

2

"What Has the Church Said?"

Scriptural and Theological Guidance on Money

M**any of the survey respondents** and focus groups referred to in chapter 1 were reluctant to discuss money in church. Yet, the church has been talking about money since its inception, and Judaism began discussing money long before Christianity. Old Testament scholar Walter Brueggemann argues that "economics is a core preoccupation of the biblical tradition."[1] The Bible contains five hundred references to prayer and two thousand references to money and possessions.[2] Jesus frequently discussed money. In fact, he mentioned it second only to the kingdom of God. By one count, 62 percent of Jesus's parables refer to money and possessions.[3] This is not surprising since he came from a Jewish

1. Brueggemann, *Money and Possessions*, xix.

2. Michael Schut, ed., *Money and Faith: The Search for Enough* (New York: Morehouse Publishing, 2008), 39.

3. Schut, *Money and Faith*, 39; Michael Packer, "Jesus Talked the Most about . . . Money?" Smyrna Patch, July 24, 2011, accessed November 19, 2016. *http://patch.com/georgia/smyrna/jesus-talked-the-most-aboutmoney*; Richard J. Foster, *Celebration of Discipline: The Path to Spiritual Growth*, special anniversary ed. (New York: HarperOne, 2018), 83.

tradition that was keenly focused on the theological and biblical aspects of money. The book of Genesis and the Psalms declare that all things, including money, come from God, and the traditions of Deuteronomy insist that money must be managed with an eye toward justice.[4] Jesus was familiar with Deuteronomy's prohibition on usury and the calls for Sabbath, a Year of Release, and Jubilee, all of which sought to free people from institutionalized debt and economic inequality.[5] Jesus also realized the centrality of money to people's lives, both physically and spiritually. Money serves as a kind of mirror that reveals who people are to the world; it provides the opportunity to demonstrate generosity and compassion or to display greed and hoarding. Therefore, money can be a source of anxiety and also, for followers of Christ, an opportunity for discipleship.

A Brief Overview of Christian Theological Views of Money

The early Christian church adapted two different and somewhat conflicting views of wealth, which might explain Christians' persistent confusion regarding the proper relationship between faith and finance. On the one hand, Jesus was deeply skeptical about money and possessions, but on the other hand, he recognized the importance of money for providing support and hospitality to those in need.[6] Biblical scholar Sondra Ely Wheeler characterizes these approaches to wealth as peril and obligation, each of which demands different behavior.[7] If wealth and possessions are perilous,

---

4. Brueggemann, *Money and Possessions*, 5.

5. Brueggemann, *Money and Possessions*, 53.

6. Luke Timothy Johnson, *Sharing Possessions: What Faith Demands*, 2nd ed. (Grand Rapids, MI: Eerdmans, 2011), 19.

7. Sondra Ely Wheeler, *Wealth as Peril and Obligation* (Grand Rapids, MI: Eerdmans, 1995), 46.

one should give them all away. But if wealth and possessions impose a responsibility, those entrusted with them are required to use their resources for the care of others.

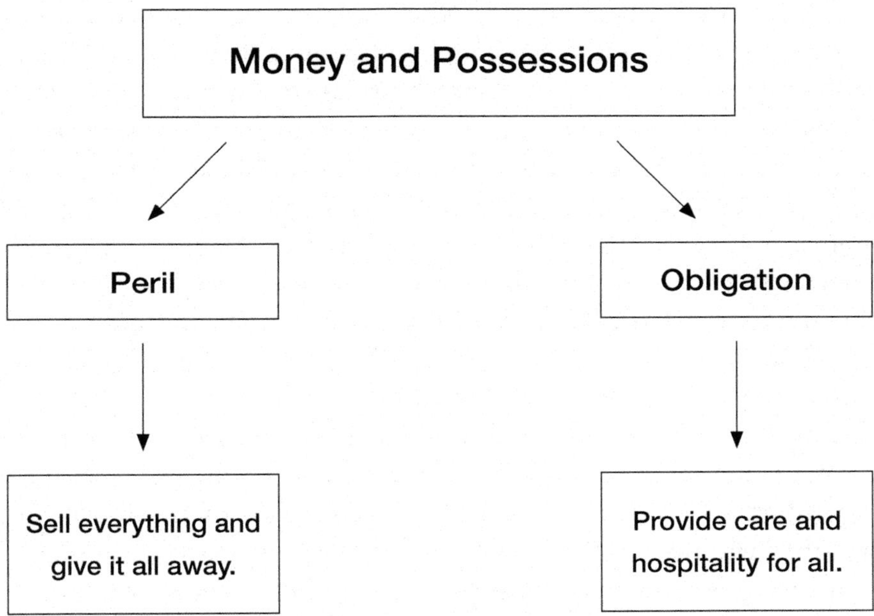

Jesus expressed both perspectives. His suspicion about money is evident in the "great reversal," when he preached that the "last will be first, and the first will be last" (Matt. 20:16).[8] Jesus's suspicion also appeared in his response to the "rich young ruler," whom he directed to sell everything and follow him (Matt. 19:16–29; Mark 10:17–30; Luke 18:18–30).[9] Conversely, he commended the rich tax collector Zacchaeus for paying back those whom he had

8. Justo L. González, *Faith and Wealth: A History of Early Christian Ideas on the Origin, Significance, and Use of Money* (Eugene, OR: Wipf and Stock Publishers, 2002), 76.

9. González, *Faith and Wealth*, 76.

defrauded and for giving half of his possessions to the poor (Luke 19:9). Jesus understood that money could be a source of redemption and forgiveness.

Jesus's views on money as both peril and obligation reflect sentiments found throughout the Old Testament. For Israel, there was a strong focus on the tenth commandment against coveting. Israelites understood that desire, which drives coveting, can be incredibly powerful, seductive, and disruptive. While the concern about coveting is articulated in the Pentateuch, the obligation to care for others is clearly articulated in the book of Deuteronomy. Brueggemann suggests that Deuteronomy calls its readers into covenant with each other, which includes "economic neighborliness."[10] Deuteronomy articulated an ethical use of money and introduced the Year of Release, which canceled all debts in their seventh year (Deut. 15:1–11), and the prohibitions on usury (Deut. 23:19–20; Deut. 24:10–13, 17; Deut. 24:14–15; Deut. 24:19–21). In addition, Deuteronomy provided a renewed focus on the needs of one's neighbor. In particular, it called for protection of the most vulnerable: widows, orphans, and immigrants.[11] Brueggemann points out that a predatory economy produces great anxiety that someone is getting something for nothing. Deuteronomy seeks to address those concerns by replacing a privatized economy with one that includes social protections for all people.[12] The challenge of economic neighborliness resonates through the subsequent books of the Old Testament.

The Psalter reiterates the ethical standards outlined in Deuteronomy. Psalm 112 specifically describes the benefits that come to the person who keeps the commandments, including giving to the poor, lending freely, and operating in justice. Psalm 112 reinforces

---

10. Brueggemann, *Money and Possessions*, 36.

11. Brueggemann, *Money and Possessions*, 49.

12. Brueggemann, *Money and Possessions*, 49.

the notion that correct behavior is supposed to create good outcomes for the individual and, more importantly, for the community.[13] Conversely, Psalm 2 warns against the dangers of greed. Psalm 49 goes further when it reminds us that we cannot take wealth with us after death. Wealth cannot provide security because security comes only from God.[14] A lack of financial security is the primary explanation that people offer for their financial anxiety. They fear that they do not have enough money to provide for themselves and their family, so they toil to attain that security. Yet, Psalm 49 recognizes that this thinking is flawed. Only God can provide security. Trusting in anything else runs the risk of idolatry.

Many of the recurring themes in a Christian theological discussion of money are rooted in the Old Testament, particularly the Decalogue and Deuteronomy. Jesus understood these themes and incorporated them into his teaching and his ministry. In the Gospels, he advocated for an alternative economy that included a set of social practices and relationships that would be consistent with covenantal Judaism.[15] In this economy, wealth would no longer be peril or obligation but a gift from God to be used for God and for God's people and God's creation. Christian notions of justice strive for the inclusion of all people and provide resources that are shared. In this radically new economy, people would avoid envy, rivalry, and individualism in favor of love, grace, and community.

While these goals might seem naive or idealistic, Jesus reiterated them in one of his most famous sermons, the Sermon on the Mount (Matt. 5–7). The sermon began by reinforcing the importance of almsgiving and the obligations of wealth. "Give to everyone who begs from you" (Matt. 5:42). But Jesus proceeded to advise his

---

13. Brueggemann, *Money and Possessions*, 99.

14. Brueggemann, *Money and Possessions*, 114.

15. Brueggemann, *Money and Possessions*, 187.

listeners to rely on God for material possessions: "No one can serve two masters. . . . You cannot serve God and wealth" (Matt. 6:24). These admonitions are not entirely consistent, and Christians have implemented them in different ways. To sort out the confusion, communities have repeatedly attempted to set standards. Some communities have focused more heavily on the peril of wealth while others have focused on the obligations. In all cases, where the standards were set in community, they were more likely to be adopted by the community members.

Community standards for wealth and possessions also appeared in the Acts of the Apostles, and they were more fully articulated in Benedict's Rule of Life in the sixth century. Yet, despite these sources, many Christians are as confused as ever about how to use it in ways that are consistent with their faith. Even with two thousand years of reflection and theology, money remains a tremendous source of anxiety. Christians continue to struggle when discerning how to use their money individually and congregationally. While a theological conversation about money will not eliminate these struggles, it will help individuals, congregations, and denominations identify those things they need to move forward and integrate money into their faith.

Theologians of most eras have discussed money. The early church embraced a preference for poverty and shared Jesus's suspicion of wealth.[16] In the third century, the Christian writer Tertullian warned, "If anyone is worried by his family possessions, we advise him, as do many biblical texts, to scorn worldly things. There can be no better exhortation to the abandonment of wealth than the example of our Jesus who had no material possessions."[17]

---

16. González, *Faith and Wealth*, 110.

17. Richard Rohr, *A Lever and a Place to Stand: The Contemplative Stance, the Active Prayer* (Mahwah, NJ: Paulist Press, 2001), 52, citing Tertullian, *The Apology in the Ante-Nicene Fathers* (Peabody, MA: Hendrickson Publishing, 1995).

Chapters 2 through 5 of Acts illustrate how Christians shared their money communally and established community standards: "All who believed were together and had all things in common; they would sell their possessions and goods and distribute the proceeds to all, as any had need" (Acts 2:44–45). "Now the whole group of those who believed were of one heart and soul, and no one claimed private ownership of any possessions, but everything they owned was held in common" (Acts 4:32).

The early church continued to share and reflect Jesus's suspicion of wealth, but it also began prioritizing the use of wealth to care for others. Paul stressed the importance of generosity in his letters to both the Corinthians and the Romans, calling upon those communities to provide financial support for the church in Jerusalem (2 Cor. 8–9; Rom. 15:26–27; 1 Cor. 16:1–4). Paul also embraced an economics of abundance in which God provides enough for everyone. In 1 Corinthians 4:7, Paul asked, "What do you have that you did not receive?" He knew that all things come from God, and therefore, Christians must use their money and resources to care for all of God's children. In Paul's worldview, whether he was describing material things or God's love and grace, there is always enough to go around.

Much like their Jewish ancestors, the early church tried to establish community standards for wealth and possessions. Community discernment and standards were crucial for adoption of financial expectations at that time, and they are equally important now for developing a shared theology of money. Without a shared theology of money, it is unlikely that individuals will change their behavior. Jesus recognized financial anxiety in the world, and he attempted to reduce it by insisting on hospitality.[18] If you are confident that church colleagues will care for you, your financial anxiety might decline. The early church understood this, and it

18. González, *Faith and Wealth*, 78.

prioritized care for the poor.[19] In addition to the Acts of the Apostles, the Didache provides one of the earliest references to shared wealth outside of the New Testament.[20] The Didache, which means "teaching" in Koine Greek, is a first-century Christian treatise that includes three sections covering Christian ethics. It is considered the oldest extrabiblical source for information about Christianity, and it provides strong guidance for sharing. Similarly, the Epistle of Barnabas, which scholars believe was written in the second century, also describes sharing wealth and possessions.[21] Finally, the second-century apostolic father Hermas, along with Clement of Rome and Ignatius of Antioch, proposed almsgiving as a means for the wealthy to share their resources and to care for the poor.[22]

As the pre-Constantinian church attracted wealthier people, its position on wealth became more ambiguous. It spoke less about the peril of wealth and more about its obligations. It focused increasingly on the ways in which money could be used for the care of the poor and for building up the church. Second-century Greek bishop Irenaeus shared his predecessors' suspicion of wealth, but he did not advocate a complete renunciation of all goods. Instead, he expected Christians to use their goods "for righteousness even while knowing that they are not rightful belongings, and even knowing that they are the result of unrighteousness."[23] Second-century theologian Clement of Alexandria foreshadowed

---

19. Peter Van Nuffelen, "Social Ethics and Moral Discourse in Late Antiquity," in *Reading Patristic Texts on Social Ethics*, ed. Johan Leemans, Brian J. Matz, and Johan Verstraeten (Washington, DC: Catholic University of America Press, 2011), 54–55.

20. González, *Faith and Wealth,* 93.

21. González, *Faith and Wealth,* 95.

22. González, *Faith and Wealth,* 101.

23. González, *Faith and Wealth,* 111.

a virtue of sufficiency: "Just as the size of the foot determines the size of the shoe, so should the needs of the body determine what one possesses. All that we possess is given to us for us, and for sufficiency."[24] As it grew, the early church moved away from the complete renunciation of wealth. Instead, it encouraged a detachment from wealth, and theologians started to develop a virtue of sufficiency. Fourth-century Greek bishop Basil of Caesarea criticized the aggressive accumulation of wealth and proposed a sufficiency test. A sufficiency test holds that individuals keep only the money and property that they need for survival and share the rest of their wealth with others.[25]

Understandably, Christians have struggled to agree on what is sufficient. What might seem sufficient to a monk living in the desert might not seem sufficient to a citizen living in Rome. In the fourteenth century, Dominican priest Thomas Aquinas argued that greed is antithetical to God. He condemned usury and wrote about the ethical pricing of goods.[26] As part of his study of Aristotle and Plato, Aquinas also reexamined the Aristotelian virtue of sufficiency.[27] Aquinas's virtue of sufficiency attempted to determine how many resources an individual truly needed, and he made sure that the same number of resources would be available to everyone. Historically, the virtue of temperance was applied exclusively to personal behavior, particularly the consumption of food and alcohol, but Aquinas also applied it to economic consumption. Aquinas's virtue of sufficiency embraced both moderation and justice, and sought to place the "understanding and

24. González, *Faith and Wealth*, 115.

25. Brian Matz, "The Principle of Detachment," in *Reading Patristic Texts on Social Ethics*, 183.

26. Thomas *Aquinas, Summa Theologica ST-II,* q. 77, art 1, accessed March 20, 2020, *https://www.ccel.org/a/aquinas/summa/SS/SS077.html#SSQ77OUTP1*.

27. Matz, "The Principle of Detachment," 183.

practices of 'enough' at the heart of a virtue-centered construal of the moral life."[28]

In the modern era, church leaders are again grappling with the idea of sufficiency as they try to discern what people genuinely need in their lives. Pope Francis reiterated Aquinas's call when he exhorted Christians to move beyond indifference, selfishness, and self-sufficiency toward a more inclusive notion of sufficiency.[29] Within the Anglican Communion, the Rt. Rev. Julio Murphy, the Episcopal bishop of Panama, has advocated for a virtue of sufficiency as the best way to overcome global income inequality and prepare for the reign of God.[30] By only using the resources needed for survival, there might be enough resources to provide for everyone on the planet. By listening to these voices, the Church has been attempting communal formation and the discernment of its standards for wealth and possessions. However, the Church continues to have a difficult time reaching consensus.

It is a particularly challenging discussion in the United States, where wealth has not only been viewed as peril and obligation, but also as a blessing. Scripture at times supports this view. Throughout the Old Testament, there are recurring references to wealth as a blessing.[31] In the contemporary United States, this view has manifested as prosperity theology, but there is nothing new about

---

28. Christine Firer Hinze, "'What Is Enough?' Catholic Social Thought, Consumption, and Material Sufficiency," in *Having: Property and Possession in Religious and Social Life*, ed. William Schweiker and Charles Matthews (Grand Rapids, MI: Eerdmans, 2004), 176.

29. Pope Francis, "Deliver Us from Indifference, Selfishness, and Self-Sufficiency," Archdiocese of Malta, November 9, 2016, accessed March 20, 2020, *https://church.mt/pope-francis-deliver-us-from-indifference-selfishness-and-self-sufficiency/*.

30. Julio E. Murray, "The AGAPE Economy: The Church's Call to Action," *The Anglican Theological Review* 98, no. 1 (Winter 2016): 126–28.

31. Wheeler, *Wealth as Peril and Obligation*, 125.

this. Starting with English and American Puritans in the eighteenth century, wealth was viewed as God's gift and reward for the righteous.[32]

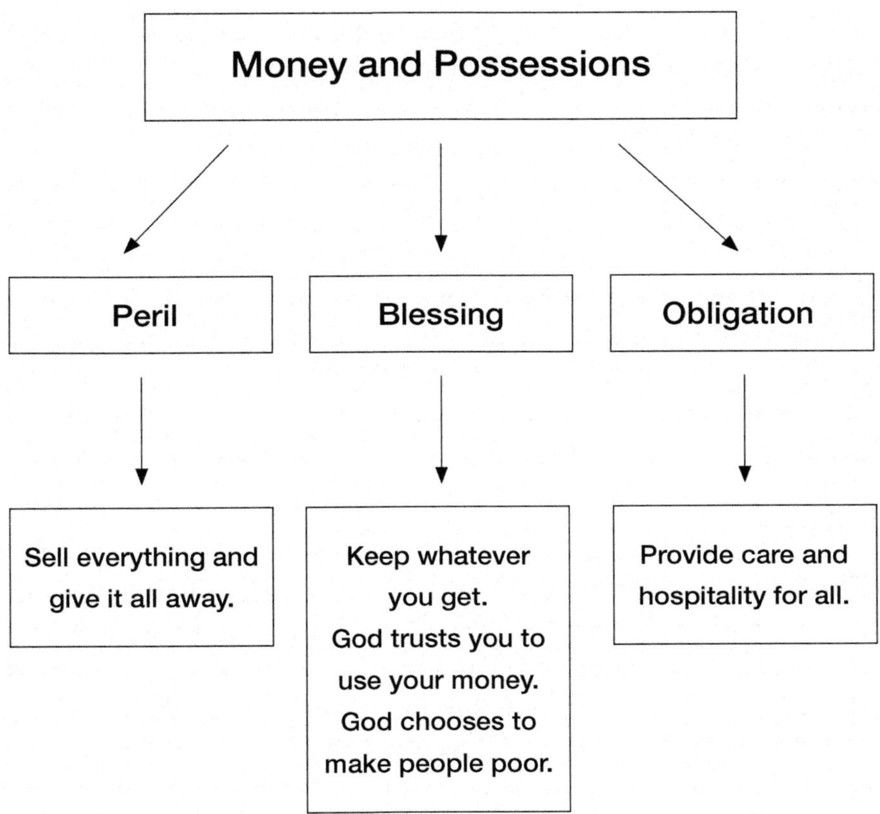

By the early nineteenth century, the theology of blessing had won broad acceptance.[33] During the early twentieth century, several

32. Eugene McCarraher, *The Enchantment of Mammon: How Capitalism Became the Religion of Modernity* (Cambridge, MA: Belknap Press of Harvard University Press, 2019), 117.

33. McCarraher, *Enchantment of Mammon*, 125, 131, 145, 147.

business leaders made enormous fortunes that they attributed to God.[34] Standard Oil founder John D. Rockefeller considered himself God's "wise and responsible steward" of his wealth.[35] He believed that God had entrusted him to use his money as only he saw fit. In the 1920s Henry Ford became an "amateur theologian," arguing that machinery was "the New Messiah."[36] Over the years, however, contrarian voices have cautioned about the peril of wealth. Social gospelers, Christian socialism, Catholic Workers, and other groups tried to return the United States to a notion of wealth as peril and obligation, but they have found little support.[37] The prevalent view of wealth as a blessing for a lucky few precludes the possibility of true community discernment over standards for wealth and possessions. Instead, the theology of money has been largely determined by those who controlled the money, thereby displacing other voices from the conversation, which explains the difficulty in starting theological conversations of money in churches today.

Sharing

Throughout scripture and Christian theology, sharing wealth and possessions is a recurring solution to the challenges posed by money. New Testament scholar Luke Timothy Johnson proposes that all of scripture demands sharing possessions, both as a "mandate and symbol of faith."[38] The Pentateuch shows a deep covenantal bond between God and God's people, and that covenant requires sharing possessions because all things come from God.[39]

34. McCarraher, *Enchantment of Mammon*, 362.

35. McCarraher, *Enchantment of Mammon*, 194.

36. McCarraher, *Enchantment of Mammon*, 362.

37. McCarraher, *Enchantment of Mammon*, 351, 353.

38. Johnson, *Sharing Possessions*, 73.

39. Johnson, *Sharing Possessions*, 81.

The Prophets and the Psalms reiterate that sharing is the only reasonable response to God's creation.[40] The Letter of James provides more explicit instruction: "If a brother or sister is naked and lacks daily food, and one of you says to them, 'Go in peace; keep warm and eat your fill,' and yet you do not supply their bodily needs, what is the good of that? So faith by itself, if it has no works, is dead" (2:15–17).

The Gospels also reiterate these guidelines. Repeatedly, Jesus mandated open-ended caring and financial support for others. In his parable of the Good Samaritan, after rescuing the Jewish victim of a crime, the Samaritan took the man to an inn where he would be cared for, and the Samaritan assured the innkeeper that he would pay for all the costs of the victim's care upon his return: "The next day he took out two denarii, gave them to the innkeeper, and said, 'Take care of him; and when I come back, I will repay you whatever more you spend'" (Luke 10:35). God gives us the gifts that are necessary for living and for giving, and God mandates that we freely share those gifts. Like Sondra Ely Wheeler, Johnson recognizes that money and possessions are a potential danger, but they are also necessary in order to provide hospitality. Johnson differs from liberation theologians because he does not see the lack of a "utopian vision or specific social ethic" as a loss, but as a blessing; it enables individuals to exercise their faith and love of God in giving to others.[41] Ultimately, he concludes that the dilemma of how individuals share their God-given possessions is "not the task of theology but of the obedience of faith."[42]

The Roman Catholic theologian William Cavanaugh argues that sharing is the only way for Christians to overcome insatiable human desire and establish right relations between God and their money. He

40. Johnson, *Sharing Possessions*, 87–89.

41. Johnson, *Sharing Possessions*, 105.

42. Johnson, *Sharing Possessions*, 106.

sees sharing as a way of maintaining a detachment from wealth and possessions so that our possessions become a tool for greater attachment to God and to our fellow human beings.[43] Otherwise, possessions can start to control us, and humans risk being consumed by their possessions, rather than the other way around. Cavanaugh suggests numerous ways to share with others: giving directly to those in need, supporting local businesses, or depositing money in banks that support local community development.[44] He does not recommend one option over another, but he stresses the importance of choosing some way of sharing. Cavanaugh's suggestions reinforce the communal nature of theological discussions of money. While we tend to think about money as a matter of individual choice, it is, in a Christian context, a matter of communal and global responsibility.

The Trinity and Money

There is another theologically grounded way to frame the discussion that incorporates both the personal use of money and systemic change to the economic system: a Trinitarian approach to money. While the Trinity historically has been identified as the Father, the Son, and the Holy Spirit, some Christians refer to the three persons of the Trinity as the Creator, the Redeemer, and the Sustainer. Could we use the framework of Creator, Redeemer, and Sustainer as a way to evaluate economic decisions?

Historically, Trinitarian approaches to money have focused largely on the communal, noncompetitive, and interdependent relationship between the three persons of the Trinity. Therefore, such approaches have guided humans to share resources, recognizing our interdependency and our communal covenant with God. Looking

---

43. William T. Cavanaugh, *Being Consumed: Economics and Christian Desire* (Grand Rapids, MI: Eerdmans, 2008), 52.

44. Cavanaugh, *Being Consumed*, 57.

at money from a creative, redemptive, and sustaining viewpoint requires more than sharing resources; it requires additional discernment. How does an individual, congregation, or denomination determine if something is creative, redemptive, and sustaining?

Creator, Redeemer, and Sustainer is not intended to replace Father, Son, and Holy Spirit but can highlight one area of our understanding of the Trinity.[45] Creator, Redeemer, and Sustainer might help Christians understand how they can spend their money in ways that are consistent with the Trinity. Ludwig Wittgenstein wrote, "Practice gives words their sense."[46] Creator, Redeemer, and Sustainer give practice to the words of the Trinity in a way that Father, Son, and Holy Spirit do not.

This approach prioritizes spending that honors God's creation rather than exclusively focusing on human creations. By doing so, we might better appreciate the material gifts that God has already given to us, which could enhance our relationship with God and make the divine presence more visible to us in the world. In Matthew 6:19–21, Jesus says:

> Do not store up for yourselves treasures on earth, where moth and rust consume and where thieves break in and steal; but store up for yourselves treasures in heaven, where neither moth nor rust consumes and where thieves do not break in and steal. For where your treasure is, there your heart will be also.

Walter Brueggemann asserts that this passage contrasts the commodities of the earth with God's true creation, and Jesus instructs the disciples to focus on God's creation.[47] Similarly, in

---

45. David S. Cunningham, *These Three Are One: The Practice of Trinitarian Theology* (Malden, MA: Blackwell, 1998), 93.

46. Ludwig Wittgenstein, *Culture and Value*, ed. G. H. von Wright and Heikki Nyman, trans. Peter Winch (Chicago: University of Chicago Press, 1980), 85.

47. Brueggemann, *Money and Possessions*, 194.

Luke 12:16–21, Jesus tells the parable of the rich man who built bigger barns but who died the following morning. The man was foolishly focused on the commodities of the world rather than God's creation.

Creation also supports economic development, despite the cautionary tale of the farmer who built bigger barns. Catholic theologian and economist Michael Novak argued that God intended for humans to be "agents of progress."[48] In his 1981 encyclical *Laborem Exercens* (Through Work), Pope John Paul II suggested that when people work, they imitate and share in the work of the Creator.[49] Creative entrepreneurs bring new products and services into the world. Novak also viewed the Roman Catholic Church as a potential mitigating force between desire and creativity. The church can provide spiritual and ethical formation and assist in discernment as people determine how God is calling each of them to use their money in ways that are both creative and consistent with God's creation. As we build our relationship with God, it is only reasonable that we would respect, honor, and seek to preserve God's creation.

Determining how to make money redemptive is more challenging than honoring God's creation. The Rev. Dr. Gawain de Leeuw, in his book *The Body of Christ in a Market Economy*, argues that forgiving debts could be a redemptive use of money. Scripture generally regards the accumulation of money as a sin because it comes at the expense of others. However, individuals redeem themselves when they give money away or forgive debts.[50] Forgiving debt can be redemptive because it might prompt the debtor to also forgive

48. Michael Novak, *The Spirit of Democratic Capitalism* (Lanham, MD: Madison Books, 1982), 45.

49. Pope John Paul II, "Working as a Sharing in the Activity of the Creation," in *Laborem Exercens* (Through Work), September 14, 1981.

50. de Leeuw, *Body of Christ*, 15.

debts owed to them. The former debtor will remember the gratuitous generosity that he or she received, along with the joy and relief that it brought. Paul applauded this approach when he described the "cheerful giver" in 2 Corinthians 9:6–8:

> The point is this: the one who sows sparingly will also reap sparingly, and the one who sows bountifully will also reap bountifully. Each of you must give as you have made up your mind, not reluctantly or under compulsion, for God loves a cheerful giver. And God is able to provide you with every blessing in abundance, so that by always having enough of everything, you may share abundantly in every good work.

Jesus underscored the importance of forgiving debts in the parable of the unforgiving servant (Matt. 18:21–35). In this parable, a king forgives the ten thousand talents that are owed to him by a slave, but the same slave refuses to forgive the one hundred denarii owed to him by another slave. Consequently, the king "handed him over to be tortured until he would pay his entire debt" (Matt. 18:34). Jesus concluded the parable by reminding his disciples, "So my heavenly Father will also do to every one of you, if you do not forgive your brother or sister from your heart" (Matt. 18:35). In his ministry, Jesus consistently stressed the necessity of forgiveness, including the forgiveness of financial debts; it is essential for redemption.

Like Paul, James also highlighted the value of such generosity. James 1:17 declares: "Every generous act of giving, with every perfect gift, is from above, coming down from the Father of lights, with whom there is no variation or shadow due to change." Once unburdened from debt, people can pursue new opportunities and create new things. They can start new businesses or buy new things. They can employ more people. They can spur on the ongoing process of creation. They can also better sustain themselves, their communities, and potentially even the planet. In the Trinity, all three persons are in a perpetual dance, which is called the *perichoresis*. So, too, creation, redemption, and sustainability are in a dance that support and reinforce each other and the kingdom of God. Debt forgiveness provides a beautiful example of the *perichoresis* in our midst.

Finally, money can be used in ways that are sustaining for both us and for God's world. Taking care of ourselves is one of the principal benefits of the Sabbath and a reason that Jesus and scripture put limitations on our spending. Jesus and the prophets recognized that worshipping the golden calf of wealth and consumerism exhausts our lives and brings anxiety rather than transforming our lives and bringing peace. Similarly, Christians could prioritize spending money in ways that are sustaining for all God's creations on the planet. The virtue of sufficiency, almost by necessity, addresses sustainability. It is a virtue to prudently use global resources so that all of God's creation and all of God's creatures have resources. Brueggemann asserts that "the great reversal is not a matter of escapist speculation; rather it is grounded in economic realism that recognizes that such disparity of wealth and poverty is unsustainable."[51] Sustainability supports God's creation, which demonstrates another way that creation, redemption, and sustainability are intertwined in a mutually supportive dance.

An overwhelming majority of the respondents to the surveys completed for this book had an interest in learning how the concept of the Trinity might be applied to money. These results were surprising since many of them had objected to conversations about money in church. Of course, the challenge is determining what is a creative, redemptive, or sustainable use of money. Critics might fear that a clever person could justify any purchase under these terms. Therefore, it is critical for a community, rather than an individual, to discern what it considers creative, redemptive, or sustainable uses

51. Brueggemann, *Money and Possessions*, 261.

of money. With standards in place, a community might be able to live into those values, just like in the Acts of the Apostles and as the Benedictines did. A Trinitarian approach to money represents one of the innovative new ways of advancing the conversation about money that might resonate with individuals, congregations, and even denominations.

CHAPTER

3

History of Stewardship

Since stewardship promotion is largely an American contribution to theological thought, it is important to know something of its history.[1]

—*George A. E. Salstrand, ThD,*
The Story of Stewardship in the United States of America

In focus groups, conversations about money and the church invariably reverted to the expenses of the church rather than to the responsibilities imposed on Christians for the use of their money. How is it that Christians see the primary application of their faith to finance in terms of how much money they give to the church? Throughout much of the church's history, the state and wealthy patrons covered its major expenses. Nevertheless, individual stewardship remained an important source of support, though it tended to focus on the care of the poor rather than the construction of churches. It also varied throughout the centuries. During the fourth century, the church was funded by the Roman emperor and wealthy Roman citizens, but it also started to attract middle-class

1. George A. Salstrand, *The Story of Stewardship in the United States of America* (Grand Rapids, MI: Baker, 1956), 11.

donors. During the Middle Ages, the church supported itself with the property and assets that it had acquired from donors and the state. But in the last two hundred years, the situation has changed, particularly in the United States, where the church has relied extensively on individual stewardship to cover its expenses. While the discussion of stewardship has increased in churches in the United States, the theological discussions of money have decreased. It seems that as the church has only a limited amount of time to discuss money, it has chosen stewardship as its focus. This chapter provides a brief history of stewardship to explain how we have arrived at the current situation.

Most Christians in the first through fourth centuries lived in subsistence poverty, and they were not in a position to offer money to the church. The considerations of sufficiency and the Trinity discussed in chapter 2 were limited to a small group of financially secure Christians. Prior to the conversion of Constantine in 312 CE, early church leaders were largely itinerant preachers who lived off the charity of others. Jesus himself, along with his disciples, depended on the support of several wealthy women, as described in Luke 8.

> The twelve were with him, as well as some women who had been cured of evil spirits and infirmities: Mary, called Magdalene, from whom seven demons had gone out, and Joanna, the wife of Herod's steward Chuza, and Susanna, and many others, who provided for them out of their resources. (Luke 8:1–3)

Generally, Christian leaders were expected to engage in "charismatic begging," which was common in Palestine.[2] This practice demonstrated the authenticity of the leader's call. It was considered to be a sign of faith that a religious leader would rely solely on gifts

---

2. Francis M. Young and David F. Ford, *Meaning and Truth in Second Corinthians* (Eugene, OR: Wipf and Stock, 1987), 182.

from others. The expectation was also based on Matthew 10:8–11, where Jesus commanded his disciples to

> cure the sick, raise the dead, cleanse the lepers, cast out demons. You received without payment; give without payment. Take no gold, or silver, or copper in your belts, no bag for your journey, or two tunics, or sandals, or a staff; for laborers deserve their food. Whatever town or village you enter, find out who in it is worthy, and stay there until you leave.

Some early Christians were even critical of leaders, like Paul, who pursued a profession in addition to their religious life to support themselves. Their profession suggested that they were unwilling to completely put their trust in God.[3] However, many who trusted in God were also completely dependent on wealthy patrons. Acts 16:14–15 describes the financial support Lydia provided to the early Christian community.

> A certain woman named Lydia, a worshiper of God, was listening to us; she was from the city of Thyatira and a dealer in purple cloth. The Lord opened her heart to listen eagerly to what was said by Paul. When she and her household were baptized, she urged us, saying, "If you have judged me to be faithful to the Lord, come and stay at my home." And she prevailed upon us.

Scripture also mentions other patrons who supported Christians. In Romans 16:2, Paul referred to the support of the deacon Phoebe. Other patrons in the New Testament include Jason (Acts 16), Artistobulus (Rom. 16:10), Stephanas (1 Cor. 1:16), Onesiphorus (2 Tim. 4:19), Philemon (Phil. 2), and Gaius (3 John 1).[4]

---

3. Young and Ford, *Meaning and Truth*, 182.

4. Greg Brothers, "Patrons and Patronage in the Early Christian Church," *Ministry: International Journal of Pastors*, July 2002, accessed January 5, 2021, *https://www.ministrymagazine.org/archive/2002/07/patrons-and-patronage-in-the-early-christian-church.html.*

Patrons became even more plentiful in the fourth century. After the conversion of Constantine, Christianity began to attract wealthier Roman citizens. However, Christian stewardship remained relatively quiet in the Roman Empire. Prosperous Christians donated money to build churches, which popped up in communities across the empire. But the costs of building these churches were modest compared to the vast sums that Roman aristocrats lavished on private residences and public entertainment.[5] As a result, these early examples of Christian stewardship have historically been overlooked, even though it now appears to have been more extensive than previously suggested by historians. Notably, fourth-century Christians made no distinction between giving money to build a church and giving alms to the poor. Both reflected a deep commitment to God.[6]

Fourth-century bishops in the Roman Empire had one distinct advantage over church fundraisers today: their parishioners had a different view of money and of giving than that of modern American Christians. In the Roman Empire, giving gifts was a societal norm that connected people together. Roman citizens were also expected to give gifts to their city and to the empire, even beyond their taxes. Many wealthy people owed their wealth to the emperor, so they felt obliged to return a portion of it to their local community and to the empire. Community giving included gifts of food and entertainment for all citizens, particularly the poor. Therefore, when bishops encouraged Christians to give to the church and to the poor, including poor people who were not Roman citizens, they found a receptive audience. As a result, when the Roman Empire deteriorated, the bishops had already built a broad base of financial support among a diverse group of donors that could sustain the

5. Peter Brown, *Through the Eye of a Needle: Wealth, the Fall of Rome, and the Making of Christianity in the West, 350–550 AD* (Princeton, NJ: Princeton University Press, 2012), 41.

6. Brown, *Through the Eye of a Needle*, 42.

church through the uncertain political times ahead. In addition, in the fourth century, wealthy Roman citizens began endowing clergy positions at specific churches. These titular churches were not dependent on a bishop or on the pope, because they had their own financial means.[7]

In the early Middle Ages, the church was acquiring and managing its own land and assets. The bishops and their clerical staffs also effectively and professionally managed these assets, and they continued to encourage lay donors. In fact, the church was one of the first institutions to introduce professional asset management. As a result, by the seventh century, the church was in a strong financial position.[8] Throughout the Middle Ages, the church solidified its wealth by leveraging existing assets and imposing tithes on its members. For example, many monasteries, like the Benedictine monastery in Cluny, France, rented their land to tenant farmers; some historians claim that these monasteries imposed a form of serfdom on their tenants. In addition, many monks and nuns came from wealthy families, who were required to make significant contributions to the community. At the same time, parish churches expanded across Western Europe. Those churches imposed a tithe on their parishioners and collected one-tenth of the agricultural produce of the local farmers.[9] Church members also paid for additional church services, like baptisms and funerals. Finally, churches paid no taxes. As a result, the church developed massive wealth, owning as much as 30 percent of the land in Western Europe during the Middle Ages.[10]

---

7. Brown, *Through the Eye of a Needle*, 247.

8. Brown, *Through the Eye of a Needle*, 530.

9. Diarmaid MacCulloch, *Christianity: The First Three Thousand Years* (New York: Penguin, 2010), 369.

10. "Why Was the Church So Powerful in the Middle Ages," Reference, April 5, 2020, accessed January 5, 2021, *https://www.reference.com/history/church-powerful-middle-ages-61234fd15059a12d*.

The parish tithing system eventually developed into a state funding system. While state funding of religion is prohibited in the United States, it continues around the world today. According to a recent Pew Research survey, 22 percent of the world's nations have an official state religion, and 20 percent have a favored faith tradition.[11] In several European countries, the governments still collect a church tax. In Austria, Finland, Switzerland, Germany, Denmark, and Sweden, the tax is mandatory. In Portugal, Italy, and Spain, the tax is voluntary. In those countries, taxpayers can direct a portion of their taxes to a special church or charity if they so choose.[12]

State funding of religion was never common in the United States. Prior to the seventeenth century, some colonies in North America provided funding for local clergy. Generally, local parishes were largely responsible for supporting their clergy. Historical accounts in seventeenth-century Boston show Congregational church members would come forward at the end of their weekly service to place their offerings in a designated collection box.[13] In Virginia clergy received a uniform salary set by the colonial government from their parishes, but the funding came from the local congregation, not the government.[14] In addition to local funding, churches in North America were also subsidized by several missionary organizations, including the Society for Promoting Christian

11. David Masci, "Key Facts about Government-Funded Religion around the World," Pew Research Center, October 3, 2017, accessed January 4, 2021, *https://www.pewresearch.org/fact-tank/2017/10/03/key-facts-about-government-favored-religion-around-the-world/.*

12. Dalia Fahmy, "European Countries That Have Mandatory Church Taxes Are about as Religious as Their Neighbors That Don't," Pew Research Center, May 9, 2019, accessed January 4, 2021, *https://www.pewresearch.org/fact-tank/2019/05/09/european-countries-that-have-mandatory-church-taxes-are-about-as-religious-as-their-neighbors-that-dont/.*

13. Salstrand, *The Story of Stewardship*, 14.

14. Salstrand, *The Story of Stewardship*, 13.

Knowledge, the Society for the Propagation of the Gospel in Foreign Parts, the English Baptist Missionary Society, and the New York Missionary Society. During the same era, the bishop of London, Henry Compton, appointed many newly ordained priests to serve as "commissary" in the colonies.[15] Once those denominations were established, many colonies also supported them through local taxes.[16] The First Amendment to the United States Constitution prohibited the federal government, but not the states, from establishing a state religion. Five of the original colonies provided tax support for clergy, and twelve required religious tests for all public officials. Only Rhode Island and Virginia adopted the model of separation of church and state envisioned in the United States Constitution.[17] Therefore, state support continued well into the nineteenth century; however, it was never sufficient for churches to forgo individual stewardship.

By the nineteenth century, churches in the United States had to adopt lay stewardship more aggressively than churches in other countries. A whole series of innovations developed to support churches. They experimented with pew taxes and subscriptions. They tried church suppers and other fundraisers. In the 1840s several prominent Christian leaders preached and wrote about the importance of individual stewardship, echoing sentiments of the fourth-century bishops.[18] Congregational minister Leonard Bacon preached about the "right use of property on Christian principles."[19] Slowly, churches

---

15. Robert W. Prichard, *A History of the Episcopal Church* (New York: Morehouse Publishing, 2014), 41.

16. Mark A. Noll, *The Old Religion in a New World: The History of North American Christianity* (Grand Rapids, MI: Eerdmans, 2002), 31.

17. Noll, *The Old Religion*, 72.

18. Salstrand, *The Story of Stewardship*, 31.

19. Bob Sitze, *Stewardshift: An Economia for Congregational Change* (New York: Church Publishing, 2016), 22.

adopted more explicit tithing. In 1877 St. Stephen's Episcopal Church in Philadelphia implemented the practice. In 1890 Chicago businessman Thomas Kane published and distributed millions of pamphlets advocating tithing. In 1895 Wesley Chapel, Cincinnati adopted "storehouse tithing" based on Malachi 3:10–12.[20] Subsequently, several tithing societies developed across multiple denominations. In 1906 Dr. Henry Lansdell provided scholarly support for the practice in his book, *The Sacred Tenth*.[21] The results were quite dramatic. A 1904 study found that tithers gave twenty-four times more money to their churches than people who contributed by other means.[22]

In the twentieth century, stewardship became a major focus of lay and religious leaders. While stewardship in the United States has declined during periods of national crisis, it has remained a regular part of religious life. Though stewardship lagged during World War I, the United States enjoyed dramatic economic growth after the war, which resulted in unprecedented support for churches, particularly for foreign missions. From 1918 to 1927 foreign mission fundraising in North America surpassed all past giving levels.[23] Several Protestant denominations, including the Southern Baptists, Presbyterians, Disciples of Christ, and Methodists, ran very successful mission campaigns. During the Great Depression and World War II, stewardship again declined, but it returned stronger than ever after the end of the war. From the depths of the Depression to the 1950s, stewardship doubled for every denomination, and several denominations saw 300 to 600 percent increases in giving.[24]

20. John H. Reumann, *Stewardship and the Economy of God* (Eugene, OR: Wipf and Stock, 1992), 54.

21. Henry Lansdell, *The Sacred Tenth: Or Studies in Tithe-Giving, Ancient and Modern* (Grand Rapids: Baker, 1954).

22. Salstrand, *The Story of Stewardship*, 44.

23. Salstrand, *The Story of Stewardship*, 59.

24. Salstrand, *The Story of Stewardship*, 95, 101, 103, 106, 109, 113, 115, 119, 121.

Stewardship has become a routine part of church life. In fact, based on the surveys for this book, it might be too regular. Many people only think of the theology of money in terms of stewardship. Some scholars have argued that stewardship and tithing are one of North America's unique contributions to religion globally.[25] However, as the history above illustrates, stewardship and tithing in one form or another have existed in the church from the very beginning. Therefore, it might be more accurate to say that stewardship and tithing have been particularly well suited for the United States because Americans have also displayed a historical preference for local solutions and individualism rather than state-sponsored institutions. Stewardship and tithing, therefore, represent a logical response. Nevertheless, this narrow focus on stewardship and tithing has limited the conversation about money in American congregations. As a result, congregational leaders have an opportunity to engage in theological discussions of money that consider topics other than stewardship.

---

25. Reumann, *Stewardship & the Economy of God*, 52.

CHAPTER

4

"What Does Scripture Say?"

Understanding the Theology of the Congregation

Chapter 2 discussed how the Bible supports a variety of theological views on money. Clearly, one can find scriptural support for divergent views on faith and finance. Therefore, rather than trying to identify the one true interpretation, congregational leaders might be better served by understanding the theology of money that is already embedded in their congregations. To effectively lead theological discussions of money, congregational leaders need to know where they are starting. In a recent survey of 211 self-identified Christians, 64 percent of the respondents identified Bible stories and teachings of Jesus that focused on money. The overwhelming majority of the respondents in a clergy survey also indicated that people in their congregations were aware of this biblical material. Since discussions of money can be hard to lead, those scriptural sources can provide one of the easiest ways for leaders to start a theological discussion of money. They expose the underlying emotions in the congregation about money.

This chapter examines some of the most consistently cited stories and teachings about money and what they might tell a leader about the congregation. In his book *The Righteous Mind: Why Good People Are Divided by Politics and Religion*, social psychologist Jonathan Haidt argues that humans make their decisions based on one of six "moral foundations": authority/subversion, fairness/cheating, sanctity/degradation, liberty/oppression, care/harm, and loyalty/betrayal. While people generally believe that they are making rational decisions, Haidt demonstrates that people actually make emotional decisions and subsequently find intellectual justification for those decisions.[1] In analyzing scripture passages related to money, Haidt's framework is a useful tool for identifying the underlying emotions evoked by each passage. Using those emotions as a guide, congregational leaders will be in the best position to understand the theology of money within their congregations and to discern a way to address financial anxiety in the congregation.

Authority

> He blessed him and said, "Blessed be Abram by God Most High, maker of heaven and earth; and blessed be God Most High, who has delivered your enemies into your hand!" And Abram gave him one-tenth of everything. (Gen. 14:19–20)

Genesis 14:20–21 provides one of the most explicit references to our use of resources, including money, in scripture. There are similar passages in Leviticus 27:30–32 and Numbers 18:21, 24, which describe the Levitical tithe, and in Deuteronomy 14:22–27, which describes annual festival giving. Yet, according to Nonprofit Source, only 5 percent of Christians give a tithe, and on average, they give just 2.5 percent of their income, which is well below the scriptural

1. Jonathan Haidt, *The Righteous Mind: Why Good People Are Divided by Politics and Religion* (New York: Vintage Books, 2012), 29, 61.

guidance of 10 percent. Even during the Great Depression, Americans gave an average of 3.3 percent of their income.[2] Since tithing is so rare, what does it say if your congregation cites this passage as an example of theology and money?

Based on Haidt's analysis of moral foundations, people who cite tithing typically respect authority. They appreciate clear rules, and this passage provides straightforward financial guidance. Out of respect for the authority of the Bible and the authority of the church, people who cite this verse might respond well to a theological discussion about money that focuses on authority. A leader might want to lead a conversation about what authority is needed to change our personal budgets or the church budget. On its surface, this kind of conversation could seem merely procedural, but it might quickly reveal emotions surrounding money and then provoke a theological discussion. Do people feel powerless over their financial situation? Do they believe that they have the authority to change their behavior?

Conversely, someone citing this passage might not be particularly moved by Haidt's moral foundations of care and fairness. This is not to say that those people do not value those moral foundations, but they might not respond to them as quickly as they do to authority. The goal of this exercise is to understand the moral foundations that are most important to people in congregations. Subsequently, congregational leaders can respond with the appropriate care and support. Based on insights garnered from a Bible passage, a leader can chart a course for his or her congregation, which could lead to a theological discussion of money. In all cases, it will lead to a better understanding of the people under his or her care.

2. "Charitable Giving for Churches," Nonprofit Source, accessed October 11, 2020, *https://nonprofitssource.com/online-giving-statistics/church-giving/*.

Fairness

> Blessed are the poor in spirit, for theirs is the kingdom of heaven.
> Blessed are those who mourn, for they will be comforted.
> Blessed are the meek, for they will inherit the earth.
> Blessed are those who hunger and thirst for righteousness, for they will be filled.
> Blessed are the merciful, for they will receive mercy.
> Blessed are the pure in heart, for they will see God.
> Blessed are the peacemakers, for they will be called children of God.
> Blessed are those who are persecuted for righteousness' sake, for theirs is the kingdom of heaven.
> Blessed are you when people revile you and persecute you and utter all kinds of evil against you falsely on my account. Rejoice and be glad, for your reward is great in heaven, for in the same way they persecuted the prophets who were before you. (Matt. 5:3–12)

For many Christians, the Beatitudes paint the perfect image of heaven; those who have suffered in this world will be rewarded in the next. People who cite this passage when referring to money envision a world of tremendous fairness. Therefore, a theological discussion of money could start with the moral foundation of fairness. Church leaders could start a conversation about income inequality or poverty, and that conversation might prompt congregants to explore their emotions about money. People might be invited to share the ways in which unfairness in the current economic system affects them. Are they worried about losing their health care or about being evicted? What do the Beatitudes tell us about those concerns? Do Jesus's words provide any relief? Do they feel any solace in knowing that others also share their concerns? The moral foundation of fairness can be a strong place to start talking about money.

> Then Jesus looked around and said to his disciples, "How hard it will be for those who have wealth to enter the kingdom of God!" And the disciples were perplexed at these words. But Jesus said to them again, "Children, how hard it is to enter the kingdom of God! It is easier for a camel to go through the eye of a needle than for someone who is rich to enter the kingdom of God." They were greatly astounded and said to one another, "Then who can be saved?" Jesus looked at them and said, "For mortals it is impossible, but not for God; for God all things are possible."
>
> Peter began to say to him, "Look, we have left everything and followed you." Jesus said, "Truly I tell you, there is no one who has left house or brothers or sisters or mother or father or children or fields, for my sake and for the sake of the good news, who will not receive a hundredfold now in this age—houses, brothers and sisters, mothers and children, and fields, with persecutions—and in the age to come eternal life. But many who are first will be last, and the last will be first. (Mark 10:23–31)

The story of the rich young man can disturb people. Is Jesus requiring everyone to sell everything to be his disciple? Not necessarily. Jesus did not require the disciples to sell everything. We know from scripture that they still had access to the house in Capernaum and to fishing boats. Typically, this passage is interpreted as one about individual discipleship. Jesus knew that the rich young man would never be able to follow him unless he sold his possessions. This story highlights that Jesus saw wealth as a potential peril. However, it seems that he did not see wealth as a peril for everyone and in every situation. Rather, Jesus insisted on personal discipleship. He wanted his disciples to be aware of those things that keep them from God. People who cite this passage might be concerned with fairness. Was it fair for Jesus to ask so much of the rich young man? What is God asking of us?

Since we cannot be entirely sure what God is asking of us, this story can evoke anxiety. To help address the anxiety, leaders might facilitate a discussion about what is fair for someone to possess. They could facilitate a discussion of the virtue of sufficiency. A virtue of sufficiency presupposes that God's abundance is sufficient to take care of everyone as long as people are willing to share. What would be sufficient for people to have, and what would it be like if they gave the rest of their money away? The challenge with this conversation is that "sufficiency" and "necessity" can mean different things to different people. As a result, a congregation might need to discern community standards for wealth, possessions, money, and sufficiency. In leading this conversation, a facilitator should be mindful that some critics worry that a virtue of sufficiency might undermine economic growth. Therefore, part of the discussion will need to focus on how sufficiency and economic growth can coexist. Uncertainty can be a major source of anxiety. By discussing this passage, people might develop more clarity on what God is asking of them.

Cheating

> [Jesus] entered Jericho and was passing through it. A man was there named Zacchaeus; he was a chief tax collector and was rich. He was trying to see who Jesus was, but on account of the crowd he could not, because he was short in stature. So, he ran ahead and climbed a sycamore tree to see him, because he was going to pass that way. When Jesus came to the place, he looked up and said to him, "Zacchaeus, hurry and come down; for I must stay at your house today." So he hurried down and was happy to welcome him. All who saw it began to grumble and said, "He has gone to be the guest of one who is a sinner." Zacchaeus stood there and said to the Lord, "Look, half of my possessions, Lord, I will give to the poor; and if I have defrauded anyone of anything, I will pay back four times as much." Then Jesus said to him, "Today salvation has come to this house, because he too is

> a son of Abraham. For the Son of Man came to seek out and to save the lost. (Luke 19:1–10)

The story of Zacchaeus is a wonderful account of redemption; it reminds us that Jesus did not totally reject wealth, and he forgave those who cheated others. He recognized that wealth can be a blessing when used to serve others. This passage emphasizes the moral foundation of fairness and its opposite, cheating. Zacchaeus repaid the people that he cheated, and he dedicated half of his possessions to the poor. For those who cite this passage, a conversation about basic economic fairness could lead to a theological discussion of money. How can we use our money in ways that are fair and that help build equity? Could the church support local vendors that focus on fair practices and redemption? The Israelites considered the forgiveness of debt to be a form of redemption. Can the church forgive any debts? If people advocate for a fairer and more forgiving economy, they can start to envision an economy that is fairer and more forgiving to them as well. Even if a more just and forgiving economy is far off, the prospect of and participation in creating change can be hopeful and fulfilling.

Sanctity

> Do not store up for yourselves treasures on earth, where moth and rust consume and where thieves break in and steal; but store up for yourselves treasures in heaven, where neither moth nor rust consumes and where thieves do not break in and steal. For where your treasure is, there your heart will be also. (Matt. 6:19–21)

This passage from Matthew appears routinely in the lectionary, and for those who cite it, they might prioritize Haidt's moral foundation of sanctity, have an aversion to degradation, and have negative visceral reactions to money. Therefore, a leader could ask them how they feel about money. Does it make them feel "dirty" or "bad"?

If these individuals see money as negative, it is not surprising that they resist theological discussion of money. A theological discussion might ask how money could be made to feel "clean." Is there a way to redeem money?

Degradation

> For the love of money is a root of all kinds of evil, and in their eagerness to be rich some have wandered away from the faith and pierced themselves with many pains. (1 Tim. 6:10)

This passage from 1 Timothy is frequently cited out of context and misquoted as "money is the root of all evil" rather than "*the love of* money is the root of all evil." First Timothy reflects both the potential for personal degradation and for the idolatry of money. The passage can also create a lot of financial confusion for Christians. If "money is the root of all evil," how are we supposed to pay our bills and feed our families? Paul was not necessarily telling Christians to ignore their financial responsibilities but to balance them with their love of God. People who cite this passage might respond to the moral foundation of sanctity/holiness. By focusing too much on money, they risk undermining sanctity because they make compromises for money that jeopardize their discipleship. This passage could provide a helpful way to discuss how God has called us to love. Jesus reminded his listeners to love God and one another. If we loved God and one another, what would that mean for how we use our money? What is the proper relationship for followers of Christ to have with money? Is there a way to use money without developing a love for it? This passage naturally leads into a theological discussion. It clearly reflects the perils of money, so it might be constructive to also discuss the obligations and responsibilities that come with money.

Liberty

For it is as if a man, going on a journey, summoned his slaves and entrusted his property to them; to one he gave five talents, to another two, to another one, to each according to his ability. Then he went away. The one who had received the five talents went off at once and traded with them, and made five more talents. In the same way, the one who had the two talents made two more talents. But the one who had received the one talent went off and dug a hole in the ground and hid his master's money. After a long time the master of those slaves came and settled accounts with them. Then the one who had received the five talents came forward, bringing five more talents, saying, "Master, you handed over to me five talents; see, I have made five more talents." His master said to him, "Well done, good and trustworthy slave; you have been trustworthy in a few things, I will put you in charge of many things; enter into the joy of your master." And the one with the two talents also came forward, saying, "Master, you handed over to me two talents; see, I have made two more talents." His master said to him, "Well done, good and trustworthy slave; you have been trustworthy in a few things, I will put you in charge of many things; enter into the joy of your master." Then the one who had received the one talent also came forward, saying, "Master, I knew that you were a harsh man, reaping where you did not sow, and gathering where you did not scatter seed; so I was afraid, and I went and hid your talent in the ground. Here you have what is yours." But his master replied, "You wicked and lazy slave! You knew, did you, that I reap where I did not sow, and gather where I did not scatter? Then you ought to have invested my money with the bankers, and on my return, I would have received what was my own with interest. So take the talent from him, and give it to the one with the ten talents. For to all those who have, more will be given, and they will have an abundance; but from those who

> have nothing, even what they have will be taken away. As for this worthless slave, throw him into the outer darkness, where there will be weeping and gnashing of teeth." (Matt. 25:14–30)

This challenging passage has elicited a broad range of interpretations. Liberty is likely to be a moral foundation for people who cite this passage. Many people see individual liberty in this passage, since the slaves made decisions about how to handle the master's money and then faced the consequences of their decisions. However, some commentators have argued that the slave who did not invest was actually criticizing the economic system by refusing to invest in it. Therefore, some people might see oppression in this passage and in this economic system. The master is setting up an intensely competitive system between the slaves that ultimately oppresses them. Our current economic system rests heavily on competition. As described in chapter 2, Jesus was an antirival who tried to move his disciples beyond competition. Frequently, in the United States, competition is justified as part of our meritocracy. In a meritocracy, it is assumed that the people with the best skills and abilities receive the best rewards. But what does that mean for everyone else? People who see this system as fair might still find themselves on the losing end of it. Some people might believe that there is no way for them to win in the current economic system. In fact, for those people, the current system might be oppressive. For them, a theological discussion of meritocracy and the current economic system could be a very good way to discuss money.

Oppression

> Come now, you rich people, weep and wail for the miseries that are coming to you. Your riches have rotted, and your clothes are moth-eaten. Your gold and silver have rusted, and their rust will be evidence against you, and it will eat your flesh like fire. You

> have laid up treasure for the last days. Listen! The wages of the laborers who mowed your fields, which you kept back by fraud, cry out, and the cries of the harvesters have reached the ears of the Lord of hosts. You have lived on the earth in luxury and in pleasure; you have fattened your hearts in a day of slaughter. You have condemned and murdered the righteous one, who does not resist you. (James 5:1–6)

On its face, this passage appears to be highly critical of wealth, but James's message is more subtle. Rather than condemning the rich, James warned against fraud and corruption. People who cite this passage are likely to respond to the moral foundation of oppression. For them, the leader could encourage a conversation about fairness and sharing. Rather than just actively or passively participating in systems of oppression, people might find some relief if they are able to share their possessions and encourage others to do the same.

Care

> The apostles gathered around Jesus and told him all that they had done and taught. He said to them, "Come away to a deserted place all by yourselves and rest a while." For many were coming and going, and they had no leisure even to eat. And they went away in the boat to a deserted place by themselves. Now many saw them going and recognized them, and they hurried there on foot from all the towns and arrived ahead of them. As he went ashore, he saw a great crowd; and he had compassion for them, because they were like sheep without a shepherd; and he began to teach them many things. When it grew late, his disciples came to him and said, "This is a deserted place, and the hour is now very late; send them away so that they may go into the surrounding country and villages and buy something for themselves to

> eat." But he answered them, "You give them something to eat." They said to him, "Are we to go and buy two hundred denarii worth of bread, and give it to them to eat?" And he said to them, "How many loaves have you? Go and see." When they had found out, they said, "Five, and two fish." Then he ordered them to get all the people to sit down in groups on the green grass. So they sat down in groups of hundreds and of fifties. Taking the five loaves and the two fish, he looked up to heaven, and blessed and broke the loaves, and gave them to his disciples to set before the people; and he divided the two fish among them all. And all ate and were filled; and they took up twelve baskets full of broken pieces and of the fish. Those who had eaten the loaves numbered five thousand men. (Mark 6:30–44)

People who cite the feeding of the five thousand are likely to appreciate the abundance in God's world and the way in which God cares for us through Jesus. They will probably respond to caring as a basis for a conversation about financial anxiety, emerging from a focus on scarcity. Therefore, it might be constructive to ask about a time when they experienced scarcity. What did it feel like to be lacking, and where was God for them? What would it take for them to trust that God cares for them? Could renewed confidence in God's care reduce their anxiety?

Harm

> He said to his disciples, "Therefore I tell you, do not worry about your life, what you will eat, or about your body, what you will wear. For life is more than food, and the body more than clothing. Consider the ravens: they neither sow nor reap, they have neither storehouse nor barn, and yet God feeds them. Of how much more value are you than the birds! And can any of you by worrying add a single hour to your span of life? If then you are

> not able to do so small a thing as that, why do you worry about the rest? Consider the lilies, how they grow: they neither toil nor spin; yet I tell you, even Solomon in all his glory was not clothed like one of these. But if God so clothes the grass of the field, which is alive today and tomorrow is thrown into the oven, how much more will he clothe you—you of little faith! And do not keep striving for what you are to eat and what you are to drink, and do not keep worrying. For it is the nations of the world that strive after all these things, and your Father knows that you need them. Instead, strive for his kingdom, and these things will be given to you as well.
>
> Do not be afraid, little flock, for it is your Father's good pleasure to give you the kingdom. Sell your possessions, and give alms. Make purses for yourselves that do not wear out, an unfailing treasure in heaven, where no thief comes near and no moth destroys. For where your treasure is, there your heart will be also. (Luke 12:22–34)

When asked about money and scripture, many people mention this passage from Luke. Those who cite it might wish that they could trust in God in the ways Jesus suggested. Jesus implied that individuals need not worry about possessions in this life because God will care for them. However, many people are understandably too anxious to trust Jesus's words completely. It would seem naive to ignore the potential harm in the world. They recognize that God expects us to exercise some responsibility for our self-care. When quoting Deuteronomy, Jesus said, "Do not put the Lord your God to the test" (Matt. 4:7). For many, it seems that they would be putting God to the test if they expected God to provide for all their material needs.

To fully understand this passage, it helps to look at all of Luke 12. At the beginning of chapter 12, Jesus discussed appropriate and inappropriate fears (Luke 12:1–12). After this passage, Jesus described the rewards or punishments that come from sharing our possessions (Luke 12:35–48).[3] While people tend to focus on verses 22 through 34, Jesus provided this guidance within a much greater context. He encouraged fearlessness, and he wanted his followers to recognize that what they pursue in their lives is what they treasure. Reading all of chapter 12 might make it easier to understand Jesus's message. Jesus understands our fear of harm, and based on his directives, he wants us to do something about it. He hopes that we would choose faith before finances.

Luke 12:22–34 is aspirational for many people. It also might reflect an emphasis on authority. What if God exercised the authority to take care of all our needs? Because God gives us free will, God does not intercede as directly as some might like, yet God is still abundantly present in our lives. What could Christians pursue instead of money? In his ministry, Jesus provided several suggestions such as prayer, care for the poor, welcoming others. Modern psychologists recommend some of these same tools. Ultimately, Jesus directed his disciples to focus on God rather than money. Could such a profound shift in focus reduce our anxiety and free up our understanding of money? Jesus and psychologists seem to agree that it could.

Loyalty

> [Jesus] sat down opposite the treasury, and watched the crowd putting money into the treasury. Many rich people put in large sums. A poor widow came and put in two small copper coins, which are worth a penny. Then he called his disciples and said to them, "Truly I tell you, this poor widow has put in more than all those who are contributing to the treasury. For all of them have contributed out of their abundance; but she out of her poverty has put in everything she had, all she had to live on." (Mark 12:41–44)

---

3. Wheeler, *Wealth as Peril and Obligation*, 67.

The story of the widow's charity is an example of tremendous loyalty, which might draw people who prioritize this trait to this passage. Leaders could start a conversation by asking people about times in their lives when they felt intensely loyal. Conversely, have they ever experienced betrayal? Have they ever felt intense loyalty to the church? What does it look like to be loyal to God? Is loyalty to the church different from loyalty to God? Does loyalty to God require an exceptional financial sacrifice like the widow's?

People might feel obligated to maintain a strong financial commitment to others or organizations to demonstrate their loyalty. As a result, their loyalty can bring with it financial pressure, which can easily turn to anxiety. For example, parents might feel the need to buy their children everything they ask for to demonstrate loyalty and commitment to them. However, loyalty and financial commitment are not the same as love. It is helpful for parents to remember the distinction between wants and needs. Chapter 1 described the ways in which mimetic desire causes people to confuse wants with needs.

This passage also seems to imply that people should give all their money to the church. In that way, the passage echoes the story of the rich young ruler. It suggests that money is a potential peril. A theological discussion of money might consider the following question: Is there a way to develop a healthy relationship with money while still demonstrating loyalty to the people and institutions that are important to us?

Betrayal

> Then Jesus entered the temple and drove out all who were selling and buying in the temple, and he overturned the tables of the money changers and the seats of those who sold doves. He said to them, "It is written, 'My house shall be called a house of prayer'; but you are making it a den of robbers." (Matt. 21:12–13)

Jesus's famous cleansing of the temple during Holy Week might be one of the strongest cases for sanctity, but for those who cite it, this passage also demonstrates betrayal. Jesus objected to the money-changers because they were cheating the pilgrims who came to Jerusalem. As a result, they desecrated God's house and betrayed God's trust. Pilgrims would journey to Jerusalem, and if they wanted to make an offering, they needed to buy the animal to offer and then give the animal to the temple priests. Moneychangers were necessary, but they took advantage of God's people. As a result, a conversation about this passage could begin with a discussion about economic inequality. Are there ways that the congregation might address cheating that occurs within its broader community? This passage could also spark a conversation about activities that might betray the church and our faith. Are there modern equivalents of moneychangers?

All these biblical passages provide an opportunity for a rich theological discussion of money. For the most inclusive conversation possible, it might be helpful to use several passages so that a variety of moral foundations are addressed. Having frank and open conversations about the relationship between Christians and their money is difficult, and leaders need as many tools as possible. The scripture passages in this chapter can be helpful, and the tools in chapters 6 through 8 can also enhance these important conversations.

CHAPTER

5

Race, Gender, Sexual Orientation, and Money

Even a quick analysis demonstrates the inequalities that persist in our current economic system. Therefore, they are important topics in any theological discussion of money. This chapter considers the interactions between race, gender, sexual orientation, accumulated wealth, and personal income in the United States. Depending on the congregational context, these identities might be a way of starting a theological conversation about money, or money might be a way of starting a theological conversation about these identities. In both cases, these conversations will help any congregation move toward the goal of more fully becoming God's Beloved Community.

This chapter does not attempt to address all areas of economic inequality. For example, there is no discussion of disabilities or of immigration to the United States. Undoubtedly, other areas have been overlooked as well. Economic inequality has touched many parts of society in the United States. In fact, I began the research for this book some years ago when exploring income inequality. I quickly realized that it is difficult to discuss this inequality in the church because most clergy and congregations are wary of discussing money at all. A theological discussion of money is a necessary first step to a meaningful conversation about income and economic inequality, globally and locally.

Given the persistence of discrimination and inequality in the world, it might be surprising to remember that scripture repeatedly speaks of the equality of all God's people. Starting with Genesis 1:27, scripture reminds us that "God created humankind in his image, in the image of God he created them; male and female he created them." In Leviticus, scripture calls not only for equality but for a commitment to care for foreigners: "When an alien resides with you in your land, you shall not oppress the alien. The alien who resides with you shall be to you as the citizen among you; you shall love the alien as yourself, for you were aliens in the land of Egypt: I am the Lord your God" (19:33–34). The theme of equality continues in Deuteronomy 10:17: "For the Lord your God is God of gods and Lord of lords, the great God, mighty and awesome, who is not partial and takes no bribe." The Psalms amplify this noble virtue: "Let the nations be glad and sing for joy, for you judge the peoples with equity and guide the nations upon earth" (67:4). Proverbs also reminds us of our equality before God, regardless of our wealth: "The rich and the poor have this in common: the Lord is the maker of them all" (22:2).

Jesus himself stressed equality in his ministry. He regularly ate with sinners and social outcasts; he included all people in his life and in his love. In fact, he summed up his own practices when he described how one of his followers should throw a party.

> When you give a luncheon or a dinner, do not invite your friends or your brothers or your relatives or rich neighbors, in case they may invite you in return, and you would be repaid. But when you give a banquet, invite the poor, the crippled, the lame, and the blind. And you will be blessed, because they cannot repay you, for you will be repaid at the resurrection of the righteous. (Luke 14:12–14)

Given this admonition, it is easy to imagine Jesus socializing and working closely with those who face discrimination and injustice today. Jesus's ministry is embodied in his call to love your neighbor as yourself (Mark 12:31; John 13:34).

Equality is also a recurring theme in the Epistles. In fact, some of the strongest language regarding equality are found there. Many early Christian congregations consisted of people with few economic resources, and Paul continually challenged the wealthy Christians to assist those in need (1 Tim. 5:10; 6:18–19; Eph. 4:28; Titus 3:14).[1] In Romans 2:11, Paul reminds us that "God shows no partiality." The theme continues in Ephesians 2:14: "For he is our peace, in his flesh he has made both groups into one and has broken down the dividing wall, that is, the hostility between us." In Philippians 2:3, Paul instructed, "Do nothing from selfish ambition or conceit, but in humility regard others as better than yourselves." More explicitly, Paul concluded:

> For in Christ Jesus you are all children of God through faith. As many of you as were baptized into Christ have clothed yourselves with Christ. There is no longer Jew or Gentile, there is no longer slave or free, there is no longer male and female; for all of you are one in Christ Jesus." (Gal. 3:26–28)

He echoed this conclusion in Colossians: "In that renewal there is no longer Greek and Jew, circumcised and uncircumcised, barbarian, Scythian, slave and free; but Christ is all and in all!" (3:11).

Despite these strong calls for equality, some passages in scripture seem to argue for inequality. The Epistles can be particularly challenging. In Ephesians 2:14, Paul appears to argue for equality, and then, in Ephesians 5, Paul apparently endorsed inequality when

---

1. Udo Schnelle, *Theology of the New Testament*, ed. M. Eugene Boring (Grand Rapids, MI: Baker Academic, 2009), 526.

he advised women to be submissive to their husbands and when he never specifically rejected slavery.

> Wives, be subject to your husbands as you are to the Lord. For the husband is the head of the wife just as Christ is the head of the church, the body of which he is the Savior. Just as the church is subject to Christ, so also wives ought to be, in everything, to their husbands. (Eph. 5:22–24)

> Slaves, obey your earthly masters with fear and trembling, in singleness of heart, as you obey Christ; not only while being watched, and in order to please them, but as slaves of Christ, doing the will of God from the heart. Render service with enthusiasm, as to the Lord and not to men and women, knowing that whatever good we do, we receive the same again from the Lord, whether we are slaves or free. (Eph. 6:5–8)

While it might be tempting to ignore problematic texts in the Bible, it is critical to confront them, put them into context, and recognize how they have been used to justify prejudice and inequality. These passages from Ephesians reflect the predominant Greco-Roman conception of household management. As far back as the fourth century BCE, philosophers considered the "household" as the most basic social unit. If the head of the household managed his household well, and the emperor managed the empire well, and the gods ruled the world well, then human life would flourish.[2] Consequently, Greco-Roman philosophers developed strict household codes, which many Jewish writers subsequently adopted. Generally, Paul did not refer to these codes in his early epistles, but they appear later. Initially, Paul focused on the imminent

---

2. Elizabeth Johnson, "Ephesians," in *Women's Biblical Commentary*, 20th anniversary ed., ed. Carol A. Newsom, Sharon H. Ringe, and Jacqueline E. Lapsley (Louisville, KY: Westminster John Knox Press, 2012), 576.

return of Jesus (the *Parousia*) rather than the peculiarities of contemporary life. Theologian Elizabeth Johnson suggests that over time Paul felt compelled to revise his earlier comments on the equality of women and slaves because they conflicted with the status quo in the Roman Empire.[3] In fact, in 1 Corinthians 12:13, when referring to the traditional baptismal covenant, Paul did not mention the reunification of women and men in Christ.[4] Furthermore, in 1 Corinthians 14:34–35, Paul required women to remain silent in church: "Women should be silent in the churches. For they are not permitted to speak, but should be subordinate, as the law also says. If there is anything they desire to know, let them ask their husbands at home. For it is shameful for a woman to speak in church." Paul reiterated this sentiment in 1 Timothy 2:11–12. Theologian Jouette Bassler, like Elizabeth Johnson, argues that Paul's change in tone reflected the status quo and particular tensions within the Corinthian community.[5] Furthermore, theologian Udo Schnelle has postulated that if Paul had taken a different position on household management, he might have jeopardized the very existence of the early Christian communities. If Christians had openly criticized and challenged the Roman norms, they would have faced even greater persecution and possibly elimination.[6]

Paul's position on slavery, which paralleled that of the Roman Empire, is equally problematic. While Paul did not reject slavery entirely, some scholars argue that he tried to modify it. He implored, "Masters, treat your slaves justly and fairly, for you know that you also have a Master in heaven" (Col. 4:1). Later in his letter

3. Johnson, "Ephesians," 579.

4. Jouette M. Bassler, "1 Corinthians," in *Women's Biblical Commentary*, 564.

5. Bassler, "1 Corinthians," 564.

6. Schnelle, *Theology of the New Testament*, 592.

to the Colossians, Paul described the virtues of Onesimus, a slave, and he later wrote to Onesimus's master, Philemon, a Christian, requesting that Philemon treat Onesimus with care and compassion (Philem. 1). Some have suggested several reasons that Paul was not aggressive about abolishing slavery. First, as a Christian, he had no power to affect a change in slavery laws in the Roman Empire, which was already starting to change the practice on its own. Second, in the Roman Empire, slavery was frequently quite short in duration and offered the former slave the opportunity for Roman citizenship. Third, during their period of enslavement, many slaves received education and training that could subsequently provide the basis for a career and their financial support.[7] Finally, as Schnelle argues, if Paul had more aggressively opposed slavery, he might have jeopardized the very existence of the early Christian churches. None of these mitigating factors makes the horror of slavery any more palatable, but they may explain Paul's blind spot on this issue.

Overall, the scripture passages supporting equality outweigh those opposing it. Nevertheless, despite these pronouncements regarding the call to equality, inequality remains rampant in the world. Theologians and biblical scholars have argued that the early Christian communities were making progress toward greater equality. But once Christianity became the official religion of the Roman Empire, it focused more on maintaining the status quo than on addressing inequality. Whatever the reasons, the Christian faith compels us to discern how to address it.

---

7. Luke Simmons, "Why Doesn't the Apostle Paul Speak Against Slavery?" Redemption Gateway, September 21, 2018, accessed November 1, 2020, *https://gateway.redemptionaz.com/why-doesnt-the-apostle-paul-speak-against-slavery/*.

Race

Numerous statistics demonstrate the wealth and income disparities between Black, Indigenous, and People of Color (BIPOC) and white Americans. These disparities are at least partially the result of past United States government policies. One of the best examples involves home ownership. Home equity is the primary way that Americans build wealth. Despite its wealth-generating potential, home ownership varies greatly in the United States. In a 2016 report on the racial wealth divide, the Institute for Policy Studies found that 72 percent of white families owned their homes, compared to 44 percent of Black families and 45 percent of Latino families. Latino families increased homeownership by 40 percent from 1983 to 2016 but still lag well behind white families.[8] Similarly, based on 2003 United States Census Bureau data, 75.4 percent of white families owned their homes, compared to 48.1 percent of Black families, 46.7 percent of Latino families, 56.3 percent of Asian families, and 54.3 percent of Native American families.[9] Without home ownership, BIPOC families face a much greater challenge developing wealth.

For BIPOC families, past government policies are a major factor in the home ownership disparity. In the twentieth century, several government programs facilitated home ownership but only for white people. In 1933 as part of the New Deal, the federal government created the Home Owners' Loan Corporation, which made approximately one million loans; however, it did not make a single loan to a Black person. Similarly, from 1934 until 1968, the Federal Housing Administration (FHA) refused to make loans to

8. Institute for Policy Studies, "Fact: Racial Economic Inequality," accessed November 3, 2020, *https://inequality.org/facts/racial-inequality/*.

9. Meizhu Lui, Barbara Robles, Betsy Leondar-Wright, Rose Brewer, and Rebecca Adamson, *The Color of Wealth: The Story Behind the U.S. Racial Wealth Divide* (New York: New Press, 2006), 34.

Black individuals or even to white individuals who lived near Black people. The FHA Underwriting Manual set up specific neighborhoods where it would not underwrite home loans. Banks and realtors understood the FHA's segregationist policies and enforced them through redlining neighborhoods, which further prevented BIPOC families from securing home loans. "Redlining" refers to the practice by which banks marked neighborhoods in which they would not make loans. These neighborhoods were almost exclusively neighborhoods with large concentrations of people of color. Research by professors Melvin Oliver and Thomas Shapiro project that African Americans will lose $82 billion in home equity in this generation and $93 billion in the next generation because of these discriminatory housing policies and their long-term implications.[10]

Native Americans have also lost their land and their homes because of United States government policies. Moreover, many lost their lives from war and disease brought to North America by Europeans. One estimate suggests that in 1400, there were twenty million Native Americans in the territory that is now the United States. By 1895 those numbers had dwindled to barely 230,000.[11] During the sixteenth century, the United States government negotiated more than four hundred treaties with sovereign Native American nations. However, starting in 1828, under President Andrew Jackson, the United States pursued an aggressive policy of relocating Native Americans from desirable farmland in the eastern United States to far less desirable land west of the Mississippi River.[12] After

10. Melvin L. Oliver and Thomas M. Shapiro, *Black Wealth/White Wealth: A New Perspective on Racial Inequality*, 10th anniversary ed. (New York: Rutledge, 1995), 154.

11. Richard Twist, "Unpacking Our Belongings," in *My Neighbor's Faith: Stories of Interreligious Encounter, Growth, and Transformation*, ed. Jennifer Howe Peace, Or N. Rose, and Gregory Mobley (Maryknoll, NY: Orbis Books, 2012), 160.

12. Lui et al., *Color of Wealth*, 42.

taking lands from Native people during the first half of the nineteenth century, the United States government spent the second half giving land away to white settlers. Under the 1862 Homestead Act, any white male eligible for citizenship could claim 160 acres of government-surveyed land in the western United States. Under the 1862 Pacific Railway Act, railroads won right-of-way access through Native American lands. In 1887 Native Americans lost additional land under the General Allocation Act, which divided reservations into individual 80- and 160-acre parcels, forcing private property ownership on Native Americans who did not subscribe to the view that land can be owned by individuals. Ultimately, many Indigenous people lost their land because they could not pay the property taxes or because they were cheated out of it by unscrupulous settlers. In 1891 the United States government sold more than 17.4 million acres that formerly had been Native American land, the equivalent of one-seventh of all Native lands.[13]

Native Americans continued to lose land and rights through the New Deal in the 1930s and into the 1950s. In 1953 Congress passed the "termination resolution," which sought to sever economic ties between the United States government and tribes. It had a devastating effect. After the federal government ceased recognizing a tribe, that tribe's land was divided between its members, and individuals were required to pay taxes on the land. Again, many sold their land or were cheated out of it by white Americans. Decades of United States policies toward Native Americans undermined any opportunity to build homes, wealth, or income.

Without property, it is difficult to build wealth in the United States. In fact, without property, it is relatively easy to end up with no net worth or even negative net worth. Net worth is

---

13. Lui et al., *Color of Wealth*, 46.

determined by calculating one's assets and subtracting one's debts, and in some cases, the debts are far larger than the assets. Between 1983 and 2016 Black families with zero or negative net worth increased by 8.5 percent to 37 percent. Latino families experienced an improvement. Between 1983 and 2016, Latino families with zero or negative net worth decreased by 19 percent but remained well above white families.[14] In 2001 BIPOC families had an average net worth of $17,100, down from $17,900 in 1998, and well below white families, which had an average net worth of $120,900 in 2001 and $103,400 in 1998.[15] Because families of color have so little wealth, their children incur more student financial debt than white students when pursuing higher education. Black students with bachelor's degrees and associate's degrees graduate with 13 and 26 percent more student debt, respectively, than their white peers.[16]

Overall, BIPOC individuals also earn lower salaries than whites. In 1999 the median family income for white families was $54,121, well above $31,778 for Black families, $31,663 for Latino families, and $33,144 for Native American families. Asian families were the only group to have higher median family incomes than white families, at $56,316.[17] Black families historically have had few opportunities to own land that could generate income and have had even fewer opportunities for high-wage jobs. Jim Crow laws attempted to relegate African Americans to a permanent underclass that could be a source of cheap labor in Southern states. They were essentially used to replace slavery with something just as limiting to Black economic opportunity. For example,

---

14. Institute for Policy Studies, "Fact: Racial Economic Inequality."

15. Lui et al., *Color of Wealth*, 3.

16. Institute for Policy Studies, "Fact: Racial Economic Inequality."

17. Lui et al., *Color of Wealth*, 77.

several states prohibited Black men from owning land. In addition, the homesteading offers that granted land to white settlers in the West were not available to Black settlers. Furthermore, some states placed prohibitive taxes and burdens on Blacks that were not placed on whites. For example, in the late nineteenth century, South Carolina required Black business owners to pay an annual $100 licensing fee, which was not required of their white peers.[18] During the New Deal, the United States government largely excluded southern Blacks from new benefit programs. Unemployment insurance and the minimum wage did not apply to domestic workers or farm workers, which were two primary professions for Black people at that time. These programs also excluded Latinos, who had started to emigrate to the United States to work in agriculture. Other programs, like the Works Progress Administration and the Aid to Dependent Children program, were also either unavailable to the BIPOC community or benefits were provided at much lower rates than for whites. A pattern of underpayment and inequality was a consistent feature of United States government policies, which made it difficult for BIPOC families to escape poverty.

Like African Americans and Native Americans, Latino Americans also face a considerable wealth and income disparity when compared to whites. Latino wealth has been affected by land grant policies favoring whites and by inconsistent immigration policies. Spanish settlers moved to modern-day Texas, California, and New Mexico beginning in the sixteenth century. These Tejanos, Californios, and Nuevos Mexicanos became major landowners and developed extensive agriculture and ranching businesses. Settlers with Spanish heritage moved in across the area that now comprises the southwestern United States. However, after Texas, California, and

18.Lui et al., *Color of Wealth*, 80.

New Mexico became part of the United States territory, Tejanos, Californios, and Nuevos Mexicanos slowly saw their property rights disappear. The United States legal system was slow to protect them, and they had to fend off white settlers who took their land. Even Hispanic military leaders such as Juan Seguin, who had fought against Mexico at the Alamo, were deserted by the white settlers with whom they had fought. Over time, many of these original Latino settlers lost their land to white settlers. Eventually, they also lost their voting rights after these new states launched systemic disenfranchisement. White supremacist thought maintained that white people had the talent and the resources that the United States required for economic development; therefore, the new states and the United States enforced systemic discrimination.[19] They made sure that the legal system would completely favor white settlers and removed the possibilities that non-whites would have equal opportunity. Without land, money, or even votes, these long-time residents of North America found themselves virtually powerless. The situation for Latinos became even more complicated after World War I. Prior to the war the United States had limited immigration policies. But in 1924 the United States created the Border Patrol. Between 1929 and 1935, Mexican Americans, including legal United States citizens, were deported to Mexico.[20] Later, during World War II, when the United States experienced a labor shortage, it created a temporary farmworker program and welcomed Latinos back into the country. However, after the war, in 1954, the United States reversed its policy again, cracking down on Latino immigrants. Repeatedly, Latinos have

---

19. Adriana Bosch, series producer, *Latino Americans*, episode 1, "Foreigners in Their Own Land," produced by Adriana Bosch, aired September 2013, on PBS, *https://www.pbs.org/show/latino-americans/*.

20. Lui et al., *Color of Wealth*, 146.

found themselves in a vulnerable position, making it difficult to build wealth.

On the surface, the empirical data about Asian wealth and income suggest that Asians do not experience major wealth and income disparities. However, those numbers are skewed because many Asians live in more expensive places in the United States. According to the 2010 census, more than half of all Asian Americans live in three expensive major metropolitan areas: Los Angeles (1.9 million), New York (1.9 million), and the San Francisco Bay Area (1.6 million).[21] Real estate owned in those markets boosts Asian American net worth. In addition, Asian Americans are more likely to live multigenerationally, so expenses can be shared by more people.

Nevertheless, Asian Americans have also confronted discrimination in the United States. In 1865 the first Chinese immigrants were hired to construct the Central Pacific Railroad. By the 1870s Chinese immigrants were a major part of farm and factory workers in California. From the beginning, Chinese immigrants were targeted with special taxes and fees that were not required of other people.[22] There were also particularly harsh immigrant laws imposed on them. During the nineteenth century, Chinese men typically immigrated to the United States by themselves, and once they were established, their wives and families would join them. However, in 1875 the Page Law restricted the immigration of women to the United States, effectively blocking the immigration of Chinese women.[23] The Chinese Exclusion Act of 1882 prohibited Chinese

---

21. "Selected Population Profile in the United States," United States Census Bureau, February 12, 2020; *https://data.census.gov*; "Asian Americans: Diverse and Growing," *Population Reference Bureau* 53, no. 2: 1–40.

22. Lui et al., *Color of Wealth*, 187.

23. Lui et al., *Color of Wealth*, 188.

laborers from coming to the United States for ten years. Over time, the Exclusion Act was broadened to include other Asian immigrants as well.

Starting in 1857 Chinese immigrants were prohibited from exercising mining rights in most western states. In 1913 the United States Congress passed the Alien Land Law, which prohibited noncitizens from owning or leasing land in the United States for more than three years at a time. Similar laws were enacted across most of the western United States. Discrimination against Asians continued into the twentieth century with the internment of Japanese Americans during World War II. In November 1942, 119,803 Japanese Americans were forced to leave their homes and businesses on the West Coast and were moved to internment camps in Idaho, Utah, Arizona, and other locations. They had to leave behind millions of dollars in assets. In some cases, they had just days to sell their homes and businesses.[24] As a result, many were forced to sell assets at a fraction of their value. Internment was not only a civil rights violation; it was a major transfer of assets from Japanese Americans to whites. After World War II, meager attempts were made to offer reparations to those who lost property and assets. However, it was not until 1998 that the United States offered any more substantive reparations. The Civil Liberties Act gave $20,000 to each survivor of the internment camps. More recently, there was a dramatic rise in hate crimes against Asian Americans after the onset of the Covid-19 pandemic. In August 2021, the FBI reported a 70 percent increase in hate crimes against Asian Americans in 2020.[25]

---

24. Lui et al., *Color of Wealth*, 200.

25. Dan Morgan, "Hate Crimes against Asian and Black People Rise Sharply in U.S., FBI Says" CNBC, August 30, 2021, *https://www.cnbc.com/2021/08/30/fbi-says-hate-crimes-against-asian-and-black-people-rise-in-the-us.html.*

Despite a history of discrimination, Asian Americans have closed the wealth and income gap with white Americans. The reduction in this disparity has also been at least partially the result of United States policies. Typically, people credit Asian American success with education. However, a recent study by Brown University economist Nathaniel Hilger found that education for Asian Americans did not change materially between 1940 and 1970. Hilger argues that white Americans became more accepting of Asian Americans during that time period.[26] Prior to the 1940s, Asian Americans had been depicted as dangerous and menacing. Yet, only a decade later, they were described as industrious and family oriented. In her book *The Color of Success*, historian Ellen Wu asserts that Asian Americans won broad acceptance because it suited both the recent immigrants and United States political interests. Globally, the United States was perceived as racist because of its treatment of African Americans. Leaders needed to discredit racism. They could point to the successful integration of Asian Americans as proof that the United States was not hopelessly racist. In addition, geopolitically, the United States needed Asian allies. Subsequently, whites upheld Asian Americans as the model minority.[27] The narrative of Asian American success reinforced derogatory views of African Americans and insulated whites from confronting racism. Government policies and priorities sought to maintain the status quo for white America, which resulted in income and wealth inequality for all racial groups other than Asian Americans.

---

26. Jeff Guo, "The Real Reasons the U.S. Became Less Racist Toward Asian Americans," *Washington Post*, November 29, 2016, accessed December 6, 2020, *https://www.washingtonpost.com/news/wonk/wp/2016/11/29/the-real-reason-americans-stopped-spitting-on-asian-americans-and-started-praising-them/.*

27. Ellen D. Wu, *The Color of Success: Asian Americans and the Origins of the Model Minority* (Princeton, NJ: Princeton University Press, 2014), 4–5.

Gender

Wealth and income inequality are not limited to race; major disparities exist between men and women. In the United States women own just 32 cents of assets for every dollar owned by men.[28] Among global billionaires, in 2018 there were only 256 women, compared to 1,952 men.[29] Women are also less likely to invest than men.[30] Female underinvestment is not new. In 1949 Wilma Soss created the nonprofit Federation of Women Shareholders in American Business (FOWSAB) to provide financial literacy for women so that they could begin to invest and exercise financial autonomy.

However, closing the disparity requires more than just education; it has deep historical roots. Generally, until the nineteenth century women did not have property rights. Any property allotted to a woman could be controlled by her husband or by a male relative. But in 1809 Connecticut gave women the right to execute wills and other legal documents, and in 1839 Mississippi gave women limited property rights, which mostly concerned owning enslaved people. In 1848 New York passed the Married Women's Property Act, and in 1860 New York passed the Act Concerning the Rights and Liabilities of Husband and Wife. Under these two laws, women were finally able to conduct business on their own, control financial gifts given to them, file lawsuits, and share custody of their children. These laws soon became the templates for women's economic rights

---

28. Janice Traflet and Robert E. Wright, "America Doesn't Just Have a Gender Pay Gap. It Has a Gender Wealth Gap," *Washington Post*, April 2, 2019, accessed November 8, 2020, *https://www.washingtonpost.com/outlook/2019/04/02/america-doesnt-just-have-gender-pay-gap-it-has-gender-wealth-gap/*.

29. Institute for Policy Studies, "Fact: Gender Economic Inequality," accessed November 7, 2020, *https://inequality.org/facts/gender-inequality/*.

30. Traflet and Wright, "America Doesn't Just Have a Gender Pay Gap."

in the early twentieth century. By 1900 every state had granted married women control over their own property. Nevertheless, it was not until 1970 that women were able to apply for a credit card on their own.[31] Women still face challenges accessing capital. Banks, venture capital, and private equity are harder for women to access than men, which limits their ability to grow their businesses, wealth, and income.[32] The significant wealth gap between women and men perpetuates overall gender inequality, which is likely to remain until the wealth gap narrows.

A growing percentage of Americans living in poverty are women. According to the United States Census Bureau, in 1968 10.8 percent of women and 7.2 percent of men lived in poverty. In 2016 13.4 percent of women and 9.7 percent of men were living in poverty. The results are even more troubling for transgender people. The National Center for Transgender Equality has found over 38 percent of BIPOC transgender individuals live in poverty: 43 percent of Latinx, 41 percent of Native American, 40 percent of multiracial, and 38 percent of African American transgender people lived in poverty in 2015.[33]

Women also still lag in earnings. In 2016 the United States Bureau of Labor Statistics found that men had substantially larger median weekly earnings than women across every age group. For people over sixty-five, men earned 33 percent more than women. For people aged forty-five to sixty-four, men earned 38 percent

---

31. Jone Johnson Lewis, "A Short History of Women's Property Rights in the United States," ThoughtCo., July 13, 2019, accessed November 8, 2020, *https://www.thoughtco.com/property-rights-of-women-3529578*.

32. Christian Gonzales, Sonali Jain-Chandra, Kalpana Kochlar, Monique Newiak, and Tlek Zeinullayev, "Catalyst for Change: Empowering Women and Tackling Income Inequality," IMF Staff Discussion Note, October 2015, accessed November 7, 2020, *https://www.imf.org/external/pubs/ft/sdn/2015/sdn1520.pdf*.

33. Institute for Policy Studies, "Fact: Gender Economic Inequality."

more. For people aged thirty-five to forty-four, men earned 25 percent more. For people aged twenty-five to thirty-four, men earned 4 percent more. For people aged sixteen to twenty-four, men earned 5 percent more than women.[34] In analyzing the 2016 data, the Institute for Policy Studies found that women made up 63 percent of the workers who earned the federal minimum wage and only 5 percent of the Fortune 500 CEOs. Overall, in 2016 women earned 81 percent of what men earned, a gap that persists across racial groups. These results are particularly troubling because census data from 2016 indicates that women had stronger educational backgrounds than men but lower incomes. According to the American Association of University Women, Black women graduate with the most debt, averaging $30,400 compared to $22,000 for white women and $19,500 for white men. However, according to the National Center for Education Statistics, Black bachelor's degree and associate's degree holders earn 27 percent and 14 percent less, respectively, than whites with the same degree.[35]

Gender income inequality is also a global challenge. A 2015 International Monetary Fund (IMF) study found that income inequality and gender inequality are directly linked. As a result, gender inequality limits economic development, economic growth, and overall macroeconomic stability. Based on this study, gender pay equality is not only morally just; it is also sound economic policy.[36] Nevertheless, inequality persists for several reasons, according to the study. First, there is still an education gap globally. Women in the United States are currently the majority of college

---

34. Iberkis Faltas, "Gender Wage Inequality: Still A Long Way to Go," *PA Times*, July 27, 2018, accessed November 7, 2020, *https://patimes.org/gender-wage-inequality-still-a-long-way-to-go/*.

35. Institute for Policy Studies, "Fact: Gender Economic Inequality."

36. Gonzales et al., "Catalyst for Change."

students, but internationally, women face limited access to education. Second, as noted earlier, women also have limited access to financial services. In many places in the world, women lack access to even basic banking and credit services. The IMF study does not offer a single solution but concludes that "leveling the economic playing field between men and women" could substantially reduce global income inequality.[37]

Sexual Orientation

Economic inequality based on sexual orientation is not as well documented as racial and gender-based inequity, but increasingly, research proves the discrimination and inequality experienced by people in the lesbian, gay, bisexual, transgender, and queer (LGBTQ+) community. In 2017 Harvard University T.H. Chan School of Public Health published an extensive survey that offered resounding evidence of LGBTQ+ discrimination. We will focus solely on the survey results regarding economic discrimination, even though the study covered discrimination more extensively. In the study, 22 percent of the survey's respondents, and 36 percent of transgender respondents, reported discrimination in housing, and 26 percent reported that they had lower quality housing in their neighborhood than in non-LGBTQ+-friendly neighborhoods.[38] A 2020 study from the Center for American Progress found similar results. In that study, 37 percent of respondents reported that discrimination had a moderate or significant

37. Gonzales et al., "Catalyst for Change."

38. *Discrimination in America: Experiences and Views of LGBTQ Americans*, National Public Radio, Robert Wood Johnson Foundation, Harvard University T.H. Chan School of Public Health, November 2017, accessed November 7, 2020, 10, 14, *https://cdn1.sph.harvard.edu/wp-content/uploads/sites/94/2017/11/NPR-RWJF-HSPH-Discrimination-LGBTQ-Final-Report.pdf*.

impact on their ability to rent or buy a home.[39] Historically, there have not been prohibitions on housing discrimination based on sexual orientation. The Fair Housing Act can be applied but only if it is based on an existing protected status. Consequently, the LGBTQ+ community has no protection. For example, a transgender woman cannot be discriminated against for wearing women's clothing, because the discrimination constitutes sexual discrimination, but she can be discriminated against for being transgender. Similarly, an LGBTQ+ person with HIV cannot be discriminated against because of the illness, but he or she can be discriminated against for his or her sexual orientation. However, some states offer protections. As of 2021, twenty-three states have banned sexual orientation housing discrimination, but those laws are relatively new and remain difficult to enforce.

The discrimination documented in the Harvard study also extended to individual income. There is no universal protection against job discrimination due to sexual orientation. Over 52 percent of LGBTQ+ adults live in states without any legal protection.[40] However, in the 2019 case *Bostock v. Clayton County* the United States Supreme Court held that Title VII of the Civil Rights Act of 1964 applies to job discrimination based on sexual orientation. Therefore, LGBTQ+ Americans can no longer be fired, denied a promotion, refused training, or harassed at work. Nonetheless, discrimination remains in this country. In the

39. Sharita Gruberg, Lindsay Mahowald, and John Halpin, "The State of the LGBTQ Community in 2020," Center for American Progress, October 6, 2020, accessed November 8, 2020, *https://www.americanprogress.org/issues/lgbtq-rights/reports/2020/10/06/491052/state-lgbtq-community-2020/*.

40. Susan Miller, "'Shocking' Numbers: Half of LGBTQ Adults Live in States Where No Laws Ban Job Discrimination," *USA Today*, October 8, 2019, November 8, 2020, *https://www.usatoday.com/story/news/nation/2019/10/08/lgbt-employment-discrimination-half-of-states-offer-no-protections/3837244002/*.

Harvard study, 22 percent of the respondents reported that they were being paid or promoted unequally because of their sexual orientation; 20 percent of respondents reported discrimination in applying for jobs and for college. Furthermore, 77 percent of college-educated respondents reported having fewer job opportunities because of their sexual orientation, and 68 percent reported being paid less than their straight peers. The figures are even more disturbing for BIPOC members of the LGBTQ+ community. In the survey, 32 percent indicated that people of color experience discrimination when applying for a job because of their race and sexual orientation. A 2020 study from the Center for American Progress found similar results. In that study, 35 percent of respondents experienced discrimination in hiring, and 31 percent reported that discrimination negatively affected their compensation, promotions, or job retention.[41]

As in the cases of race and gender inequality, inequality based on sexual orientation is deeply rooted in this country. Historically, United States policies outlawed same-sex relationships. In 1779 Virginia Governor Thomas Jefferson proposed castration for people engaged in the act of sodomy, and his view was the compassionate one. At the time, the death penalty was common for anyone engaged in sodomy. This punitive trend continued into the twentieth century. In 1948 Congress enacted the first federal law prohibiting sodomy in the District of Columbia, which came with a penalty of up to ten years in jail and a $1,000 fine.[42] In 1950 Congress passed the Uniform Code of Military Justice, which prohibited United States military personnel from participating in same-sex relationships; the

41. Gruberg, Mahowald, and Halpin, "The State of the LGBTQ Community in 2020."

42. George Painter, "The Sensibilities of Our Forefathers: The History of Sodomy Laws in the United States," Sodomy Laws, January 31, 2005, accessed November 9, 2020, *http://www.glapn.org/sodomylaws/sensibilities/districtofcolumbia.htm.*

code equated same-sex intercourse with bestiality.[43] Throughout most of modern psychiatry, same-sex relationships were deemed a mental illness. It was not until 1973 that the American Psychiatric Association (APA) began to realize its error, removing homosexuality from the *Diagnostic and Statistical Manual of Mental Disorders* (*DSM*-II). Subsequently, the APA began to advocate for LGBTQ+ protections.[44] It was not until 2003 that the Supreme Court, in *Lawrence v. Texas*, decriminalized same-sex intercourse.[45] Since then, the Supreme Court has recognized additional LGBTQ+ protections, despite efforts by many states to block these protections. With such a history, it is not surprising that LGBTQ+ inequality has continued to persist.

Theological Response

The statistical evidence is overwhelming; inequality remains rampant in the United States. In response, numerous theologians have attempted to prioritize the biblical directives listed at the beginning of the chapter, and they have developed strong arguments for why Christians are called to address all form of inequality. Within the Episcopal Church, the Baptismal Covenant commits its members to "seek and serve Christ in all persons, loving your neighbor as yourself" and to "strive for justice and peace among all people, and respect the dignity of every human being."[46]

---

43. "Key Dates in U.S. Military LGBT Policy," *Naval History Blog*, U.S. Naval Institute, March 28, 2018, accessed November 9, 2020, *https://www.navalhistory.org/2018/03/26/key-dates-in-u-s-military-lgbt-policy*.

44. "The American Gay Rights Movement," ThoughtCo., accessed November 9, 2020, *https://www.thoughtco.com/american-gay-rights-movement-721309*.

45. "The American Gay Rights Movement," ThoughtCo.

46. *Book of Common Prayer* (New York: Church Publishing, 2007), 305.

The Church has a critical role to play in restoring justice for God's people. Human equality in the eyes of God demands that the Church lead these conversations and advocate for greater equality. As all the statistics throughout this chapter demonstrate, tremendous economic inequality still exists in the United States. To start that work, Christians need to first be able to talk about money in church. Scripture, statistics, and theology point to the need for a theological discussion of money. We need to reflect on this history, the statistics, and the ongoing ways in which inequality continues in the Church and in the United States. These issues require some deep soul-searching in preparation for these conversations, which will help us all understand inequality more fully. These conversations can be challenging. They require patience, compassion, and mostly faith. How is God calling us to address historical prejudice and inequality? The next three chapters provide tools for congregational leaders to begin these discussions.

CHAPTER

6

Year A

Budget Planning and Estate Planning for Personal Discipleship

Starting a theological conversation about money is difficult. When money is discussed in church, people generally shift the conversation to stewardship. In my own parish I lead a discussion about how Christians are called to use their money. People immediately talked about how they determine the amount they are going to pledge to the parish each year. They had difficulty seeing that Christians might be called to use money differently in their daily lives than non-Christians. As a result, it has been challenging to steer our conversations toward discipleship and ministry. A theological conversation about money can be easier when a congregation understands the complex mix of emotions surrounding money. In one setting parishioners explained that it was easier for them to talk about money when they had a connection to the project for which they were donating the money. For example, people are far more comfortable talking about the money that they give to a church if they know how that money is being used.

Traditionally, congregational leaders have only discussed money during their stewardship season, and even then, they generally do so with some reluctance. Surprisingly, a recent survey of clergy found that many felt comfortable talking about money in their congregations, but they did not have the tools to advance those conversations. Unfortunately, there are few tools outside of stewardship programming to guide leaders in offering financial leadership. Parish leadership needs pastoral and liturgical plans that start a dialogue around money, which needs to become a normalized part of our faith discussion, along with topics such as death, illness, and sexuality. This work is also intended as a way to ultimately lead larger discussions of economic justice. Among the many things highlighted by the Covid-19 pandemic was economic inequality. Yet, to have any conversation about economic justice, we need to feel comfortable talking about money, which is the goal of these programs. If people can start to talk about their own money, they might eventually be able to talk about how their economic choices affect others. They might be able to see how the current economic system affects them and others. While these programs are primarily pastoral, their ultimate goal is justice.

This chapter and the next two present three plans, each of which includes a series of sermon notes, coffee hour forums, and group exercises. The primary focus of the curricula is the group exercises, which offer alternative approaches to a theological discussion of money. Ultimately, participants will develop new "rules," their own Rules of Life for money, similar to St. Benedict's Rule of Life. Most importantly, the curricula seek to empower congregational leaders to develop their own exercises that would be most effective in their context. Talking theologically about money will require adaptive changes to our congregations.

The sample curricula are based on the Revised Common Lectionary for Years A, B, and C. Year A focuses on personal discipleship and considers the ways in which Christians use and understand money in light of their faith. Individuals will be invited into two different sessions. The first option discusses estate planning, helping participants evaluate how their wills and estates reflect their faith and desired legacy. The second option focuses on personal budgeting. A leader might offer both sessions simultaneously or only the session that seems better suited to the congregation. For example, in an older congregation, wills and estate planning might be more relevant, whereas in a younger congregation, personal budgeting might be a better fit. While Year A exercises start as technical exercises covering wills, estates, and personal budgeting, the ultimate goal is for participants to develop a new appreciation of the choices they make with money.

Year B focuses on corporate ministry and considers the ways in which worship and parish life reflect an understanding of money in light of faith. Participants will be invited to two different sessions. The first explores a narrative budget process. Rather than starting with a spreadsheet, the narrative budget starts with a conversation about congregational priorities. It requires a congregation to describe its expenses, rough percentages of money, and time dedicated to its various ministries. This process might call into question how resources are committed in the parish. For example, how big should a flower budget be relative to an outreach budget? The second session considers socially responsible investing. This form of investing considers whether specific investments should be excluded from a portfolio, how much oversight the investors would like to have with the companies in which they invest, and the community impact of their investments.[1] Both sessions provide an opportunity for group discernment regarding the use of community assets and the development of overt community standards. While Year A's exercises encourage individuals to develop personal money rules, Year B's exercises enable congregations to develop communal money rules.

---

1. James W. Murphy, ed., *Faithful Investing: The Power of Decisive Action and Incremental Change* (New York: Church Publishing, 2019), 12.

Year C focuses on global mission and helps congregations design money rules that span the globe. Specifically, it explores how liberation theology can guide the actions of churches in the Anglican Communion. As part of Year C, each congregation will develop a plan for resource sharing with other congregations. Individual church members will be invited to two different sessions. The first session deconstructs the current congregational model, which forces every congregation to operate as an independent business. This session includes an exercise to evaluate how changes to the congregational model could enable a particular church to partner with other churches in the area. The second session offers a more global focus by discussing how resource sharing could affect the broader Episcopal Church and the entire Anglican Communion. Ultimately, each congregation will discern a project that considers its money rules.

Curriculum for Year A: Personal Discipleship, Talking About Our Money

The pastoral plan for Year A includes four Sunday sermons and eight Sunday forums about money based on the scripture readings of the Revised Common Lectionary (RCL) for Pentecost weeks 2 through 5, Year A. The Sunday forums offer two options: (1) wills and estate planning and (2) personal budgeting and financial planning. The gospel passages assigned for these Sundays are well suited for discussions on money, but money could be discussed on many other Sundays of the year too. For this pastoral plan to be most effective, it is important to separate this program from a congregation's annual stewardship program.

Pentecost Week 2, Year A: Sermon Plan

For Pentecost week 2, the designated Gospel is Matthew 9:35–10:23. A sermon could focus on Matthew 10:9–10: "Take no gold, or silver, or copper in your belts, no bag for your journey, or two tunics, or sandals, or a staff." In this passage, Jesus sent the disciples out into the world, seemingly with nothing, which speaks to the heart of people's biggest fear about money—that they do not have enough. He helped his disciples develop a detachment from wealth and possessions so that their fears would not hold them back from their ministry. This gospel passage provides an opportunity for a preacher to remind his or her congregation that Jesus talked about money frequently and that money is a recurring topic throughout all of scripture. A preacher can build on this theme by highlighting the more than two thousand references to money, poverty, and justice in the Bible, along with the recurring biblical command, "Be not afraid."[2] Jesus meant for us to "be not afraid" in all parts of our lives and ministries but especially in financial matters.

Pentecost Week 2, Year A: Option 1 Forum and Exercise

The first option for the Sunday forum in Pentecost week 2 tackles two taboos: money and death. This forum reviews the fundamentals of estate planning. The Book of Common Prayer says:

> The Minister of the Congregation is directed to instruct the people, from time to time, about the duty of Christian parents to make prudent provisions for the well-being of their families, and of all persons to make wills, while they are in health, arranging for

2. Marek P. Zabriskie, ed., *The Social Justice Bible Challenge: A 40 Day Bible Challenge* (Cincinnati, OH: Forward Movement, 2017), 5.

> the disposal of their temporal goods, and not neglecting, if they are able, to leave bequests for religious and charitable uses.[3]

Congregational leaders are expected to encourage members of their congregations to do estate planning. Depending on the congregation, people might already have wills in place and have done complex estate planning. The first session provides an overview of estate planning from a local wills and estates lawyer. Wills and estates is a fruitful way to start to talk about money because it is a pragmatic discussion. Much of wills and estate planning is focused on tax planning and legal requirements. Nevertheless, it also provides an opening for a theological discussion of money and death. Drafting a will or revising an existing will begs the question of how we live out discipleship with our money. Therefore, much of the focus of these sessions is on discerning the ways in which our faith is reflected in our wills and estate plans. During each of the four sessions, participants will also be encouraged to keep a "money memoir."[4] In a money memoir, similar to a personal journal, a person writes about her or his memories of money. Dr. Kate Levinson, a psychotherapist who specializes in money-related issues, has found that writing a money memoir is one of the most effective strategies for working through financial issues. In many cases, it is a necessary first step before people can even begin to talk openly about money. This work should empower individuals to envision how their money might aid Christ's vision of the Beloved Community. Ultimately, the money memoir will also serve as the basis for developing a personal rule of money. Individuals will be encouraged to write about how discussions about money and estate planning affect them and to reflect on why they react as they do to the topic. Are they wrestling with concerns about their own legacy or their own mortality?

---

3. *Book of Common Prayer*, 445.

4. Kate Levinson, *Emotional Currency: A Woman's Guide to Building a Healthy Relationship with Money* (Berkeley, CA: Celestial Arts, 2011), 41–53.

Pentecost Week 2, Year A: Option 2 Forum and Exercise

The second option for the Sunday forum during Pentecost week 2 focuses on personal budgeting and financial planning. The Book of Common Prayer says, "The Minister of the Congregation is directed to instruct the people, from time to time, about the duty of Christian parents to make prudent provisions for the well-being of their families."[5]

While this rubric has largely been applied to wills and estates, it also suggests a basic level of budgeting and financial planning that is required of parents so that they can provide for the well-being of their children. In the Lord's Prayer, we ask God to "forgive us our debts, as we also have forgiven our debtors" (Matt. 6:12). The original Greek translation contemplated both monetary and non-monetary debts. These references point to the importance of budgeting and financial management within the history of the church and Christian theology.

Jesus recognized that debt held people in bondage; therefore, he advocated for the forgiveness of debts, which was also required under the terms of the Jubilee. The Rev. Dr. Gawain de Leeuw points out that "forgiveness of debt is not merely a recalibration of mutual obligation, but a way of restoring the life force outside of market driven realities."[6] The Pastoral Epistles (1 and 2 Timothy, Titus) contain several references to proper management of families and congregations, including money management.[7] The word *economics* has its root in the Greek word *oikos*, which means "household," and the early understanding of economics was rooted in management of the household. *Oikos* was also extended to communities and congregations. Households, communities, and congregations all

5. *Book of Common Prayer*, 445.

6. de Leeuw, *Body of Christ*, 33.

7. Brueggemann, *Money and Possessions*, 239, 242.

need sound management. Paul makes the point starkly in 1 Timothy 3:4–5 when describing a bishop: "He must manage his own household well, keeping his children submissive and respective in every way—for if someone does not know how to manage his own household, how can he take care of God's church?"

During the first week of this program, a financial planner presents the basics of personal financial management. Participants will be encouraged to track their spending, to keep a money memoir, and to record their emotions about keeping track of their spending and the prospect of maintaining a budget.

Pentecost Week 3, Year A: Sermon Plan

On Pentecost week 3, the appointed gospel is Matthew 10:24–39. A sermon could focus on Matthew 10:29–31: "Are not two sparrows sold for a penny? Yet not one of them will fall to the ground apart from your Father. And even the hairs on your head are all counted. So, do not be afraid; you are of more value than many sparrows." This passage addresses the theme of fear that was discussed in the Pentecost 2 sermon and forum. But this week, the sermon could introduce new ways of looking at money to move beyond fear. How could we change our lifestyles in ways that more fully reflect the gospel and reduce financial anxiety? Spiritual director Barbara Wilder points to the connection that the Celts saw between gold and the divine, and she suggests that money has an energy all its own, which can be used for good or ill. She describes ways in which money can be reinterpreted as love.[8] Bishop Julio E. Murray looks at money through the lens of "an ethic of sufficiency."[9] Murray asks us to question what we need to survive and what we might do with our excess resources. Similarly, best-selling author Brené Brown has also raised questions

8. Barbara Wilder, *Money Is Love: Reconnecting to the Sacred Origins of Money* (Santa Fe, NM: Wild Ox Press, 2010), 12–18.

9. Murray, "The AGAPE Economy," 126–28.

of sufficiency in her book *The Gift of Imperfection.*[10] A preacher might include these examples in a sermon to demonstrate how one moves beyond fear by taking control of one's money and ultimately using it for the care of others and for the health of the people of God.

Pentecost Week 3, Year A: Option 1 Forum and Exercise

The forums for Pentecost week 3 challenge individuals to think about how their lifestyles reflect their faith. Specifically, the first option emphasizes the importance of clarifying the priorities that individuals would like reflected in their wills and includes an introduction to developing new money rules. This exercise has been developed from "A Framework for Rule-Crafting Practice," authored by Jane Patterson and Steven Tomlinson at Seminary of the Southwest.[11] Patterson and Tomlinson argue that habits are anchored in our core assumptions and unspoken biases. At times, those habits can limit or even contradict our beliefs. Therefore, they suggest choosing one habit in our life and examining its consequences to our faith. They frame this thought experiment with a matrix considering one's behavior and belief in the present and as a future possibility. This rule-crafting practice can facilitate discernment regarding financial matters.

	The Present	The Possibility
Behavior		
Belief		

10. Brené Brown, *The Gifts of Imperfection: Let Go of Who You Think You're Supposed to Be and Embrace Who You Are* (Center City, MN: Hazelden Publishing, 2010), 83.

11. Jane Patterson and Steven Tomlinson, "A Framework for Rule-Crafting Practice," Seminary of the Southwest, 2018, 1.

Patterson and Tomlinson illustrate the utility of this matrix with an example: Mark is a man who feels sluggish and foggy most of the time because he only sleeps four hours per night. Using the rule-crafting matrix, they can help Mark evaluate his sleep patterns, leading him through a theological discussion of sleep. The exercise starts with the individual's present behavior. Mark sleeps only four hours per night.

	The Present	The Possibility
Behavior	Sleeps about four hours per night.	
Belief		

Next, the matrix challenges Mark to identify the belief that supports that habit. Mark concludes that sleep is a waste of time. However, he also knows that he feels sluggish and foggy most of the time. The exercise requires him to consider what it might be like if he permitted himself more sleep. He realizes that he could feel rested and refreshed if he slept more. After careful discernment, Mark identifies his underlying belief and contemplates a different possible behavior.

	The Present	The Possibility
Behavior	Sleeps about four hours per night.	I could be rested, refreshed.
Belief	Sleep is a waste of time.	

Now Mark reflects on overlooked aspects of his beliefs or considers entirely new beliefs. For example, rather than viewing sleep as a waste of time, he could view it as a gift from God. In his 2009 encyclical *Caritas in Veritate* (Charity in Truth), Pope Benedict XVI argues that "rest puts our lives in perspective and motivates us for the true purpose of our ends: concern for each other."[12]

	The Present	The Possibility
Behavior	Sleeps about four hours per night.	I could be rested, refreshed.
Belief	Sleep is a waste of time.	Sleep is a gift from God.

In this exercise, Mark has identified a limiting belief (i.e., "Sleep is a waste of time"). As long as he continues to believe this, he will not change his habit. However, if Mark starts to appreciate sleep's refreshing properties as a gift from God, he might be able to adopt a new rule and change his habit. Ultimately, after reflecting on his beliefs and behavior, Mark might conclude, "Each night when I finally lie down to sleep, I will offer a prayer of thanks for the gift and accept it graciously."[13] As a result, the rule-crafting exercise empowers Mark to change his behavior. This same rule-crafting practice can be applied to any area of life. For this program, we will use it to discern new money rules.

In the following week, people will have an opportunity to articulate some of their rules around money. They could write about these beliefs and practices in their money memoirs, and the following Sunday the group will run the rule-crafting practice to develop money rules for themselves.[14] They could use this

12. Benedict XVI, *Caritas in Veritate* (Vatican City: Libreria Editrice Vaticana, 2009), 3.35.

13. Patterson and Tomlinson, "A Framework for Rule-Crafting Practice," 9.

14. Patterson and Tomlinson, "A Framework for Rule-Crafting Practice," 4–6.

matrix to examine their current money beliefs and behaviors. For example, they might want to consider the tension between their desire for security and for sharing with others. They might believe that they must provide for their family, and then they identify the resulting behavior. After discernment and prayer during the week, individuals are likely to see new possibilities for their behavior. Working through the rule-crafting practice independently will prepare them for the next week, when the group will work on this exercise together.

	The Present	The Possibility
Behavior	Prioritizing personal security	
Belief	I must provide for my family.	Sharing vs. idolatry

Pentecost Week 3, Year A: Option 2 Forum and Exercise Plan

The second option for the forum on Pentecost week 3 offers people the opportunity to consider their own lifestyles. Specifically, the forum focuses on developing priorities that individuals would like reflected in their budgets and spending. As part of this exercise, they are introduced to the money habits and rules, as described earlier.[15]

During the following week, participants are invited to examine their rules around money. They will be asked to write about these rules in their money memoirs, and the following Sunday, the group will run the rule-crafting practice so that they can develop

15. Patterson and Tomlinson, "A Framework for Rule-Crafting Practice," 1.

money rules for themselves.[16] The matrix might be useful to evaluate current budgeting beliefs and behaviors. This week might also provide an opportunity to look at spending habits. For example, are participants spending every paycheck, unable to deposit any money into savings? Looking at behavior and financial choices, their underlying belief might be that there is barely enough money to go around.

	The Present	The Possibility
Behavior	Spend every paycheck.	
Belief	There is never enough.	

However, they might contrast this belief with the numerous times when Jesus told people there was more than enough for everyone.

> Therefore I tell you, do not worry about your life, what you will eat or what you will drink, or about your body, what you will wear. Is not life more than food, and the body more than clothing? Look at the birds of the air; they neither sow nor reap nor gather into barns, and yet your heavenly Father feeds them. Are you not of more value than they? And can any of you by worrying add a single hour to your span of life? And why do you worry about clothing? Consider the lilies of the field, how they grow; they neither toil nor spin, yet I tell you, even Solomon in all his glory was not clothed like one of these. But if God so clothes the grass of the field, which is alive today and tomorrow is thrown into the oven, will he not much more clothe you—you

16. Patterson and Tomlinson, "A Framework for Rule-Crafting Practice," 4–6.

of little faith? Therefore do not worry, saying, "What will we eat?" or "What will we drink?" or "What will we wear?" For it is the Gentiles who strive for all these things; and indeed your heavenly Father knows that you need all these things. But strive first for the kingdom of God and his righteousness, and all these things will be given to you as well.

So do not worry about tomorrow, for tomorrow will bring worries of its own. Today's trouble is enough for today. (Matt. 6:25–34)

What would it look like if the participants fully trusted in what Jesus said in Matthew 6? Would it change their behavior? Could they incorporate saving into their money rules if they believed that their other needs would be taken care of?

	The Present	The Possibility
Behavior	Spend every paycheck.	
Belief	There is never enough.	Matt. 6:25–34

Talking about money is always sensitive, but it is particularly sensitive for people who do not have enough income to meet their basic needs. In 2019 slightly over 10 percent of the US population lived below the national poverty level, according to the United States Census Bureau.[17] Given the high cost of housing in most metropolitan areas, housing costs alone might be the reason that people are unable to keep a budget, which could lead to an entirely different matrix based on the behavior that housing requires the majority of their income.

17. Semega et al., "Income and Poverty in the United States: 2019."

	The Present	The Possibility
Behavior	Majority of income on rent	
Belief		

This exercise will help them explore that choice. What belief is guiding that behavior? Are they worried about their safety if they live in a different neighborhood? Are they trying to access the best education for their children? How are their beliefs aligned with their financial choices? What other options might be a closer fit? Would they like to alter their behavior by embracing the virtue of sufficiency? What are the possibilities?

	The Present	The Possibility
Behavior	Majority of income on rent	
Belief		Virtue of sufficiency

Pentecost Week 4, Year A: Sermon Plan

On Pentecost week 4, the appointed gospel is Matthew 10:40–42. A sermon could focus on verse 42: "Whoever gives even a cup of cold water to one of these little ones in the name of a disciple—truly I tell you, none of these will lose their reward." This passage foreshadows the message of mutuality in Matthew 25, and it provides an excellent basis for a sermon on the importance of sharing our assets, both during our lives and in our wills. After two weeks of addressing the personal and emotional aspects of money, this gospel passage offers an opportunity to discuss the social implications of money. Using the materials in chapter 4, a leader could discuss economic injustice, specifically the impact of race, gender, and sexual orientation on wealth and money. This week's sermon could start that conversation and foreshadow additional work that the congregation might do to address economic injustice.

Pentecost Week 4, Year A: Option 1 Forum and Exercise

The forum for Pentecost week 4 will build on the prior week's rule-crafting practice, but this week the rule-crafting relates specifically to money.[18] Patterson and Tomlinson give another example of rule-crafting: a woman is challenged by Jesus's command to "give to everyone who asks you" (Luke 6:30).[19] Consequently, she started her discernment with the possibility of living out that gospel directive.

	The Present	The Possibility
Behavior		"Give to everyone who asks."
Belief		

In her process of discernment, she realized that during her childhood her parents always worried about having enough money. Her family's fear of scarcity had shaped her beliefs. Because of her own fear of scarcity, she discovered that she was not willing to listen to homeless people who approached her on the street. She assumed that they would want money from her, and she did not believe that she had enough, so she simply ignored them.

18. Patterson and Tomlinson, "A Framework for Rule-Crafting Practice," 1–2.

19. Patterson and Tomlinson, "A Framework for Rule-Crafting Practice," 6–8.

	The Present	The Possibility
Behavior	Not listening, even before an ask	"Give to everyone who asks."
Belief	Things are scarce; there is not enough.	

After evaluating the matrix, she began to think about how to reconcile her behavior and beliefs with Luke 6:30. She resolved to take a risk and to listen to the people who approached her.

	The Present	The Possibility
Behavior	Not listening, even before an ask	"Give to everyone who asks."
Belief	Things are scarce; there is not enough.	

As she started to listen to more people, she discovered that most people did not actually want money from her. Many simply needed someone to listen to them. As a result, she concluded that, in fact, she did have enough to share with everyone who approached her.

	The Present	The Possibility
Behavior	Not listening, even before an ask	"Give to everyone who asks."
Belief	Things are scarce; there is not enough.	I have enough to share.

Subsequently, she developed a new rule for herself: "I will give my attention to everyone who asks."[20] In this case, what began as a concern about scarcity and money turned into a practice of openness and abundance. During this week's forum, invite participants to adopt the same process to reevaluate their approach to money. Do they have a belief or money rule that is inconsistent with the gospel? What does "giving to everyone" mean to them? What did Jesus mean when he told the disciples to give a "cup of cold water to one of these little ones"?

For this week's forum, the rule-crafting exercise can also be applied to wills and estate planning. It might begin with the following directive from the Book of Common Prayer: "to leave bequests for religious and charitable uses."[21] The prayer book directive is consistent with Jesus's call to care for our neighbors.

	The Present	The Possibility
Behavior		Religious and charitable bequest
Belief		Love God and neighbors.

How does that directive materialize in the lives of the forum participants? People might have a narrow focus to their wills and estate planning. For example, they might have simply presumed that they would give their wealth to their children, which might be rooted in well-intentioned concern. They might have written their wills when their children were young. However, what if their children are adults and are self-sufficient? This exercise invites the

20. Patterson and Tomlinson, "A Framework for Rule-Crafting Practice," 10.

21. *Book of Common Prayer*, 445.

participants to reconsider their priorities and to potentially restructure their wills in ways that more fully reflect their faith.

	The Present	The Possibility
Behavior	I'm giving it all to my kids.	Religious and charitable bequest
Belief	Nothing is more important than my kids.	Love God and neighbors.

The result of this exercise could be that people see that caring for their children in their wills and providing for religious and charitable organizations are not mutually exclusive. They might develop a new rule that they will give as much to charity as they will leave to their children. Jesus's commandment to love God and love our neighbors includes one's children, as well as all of God's children. During this exercise, the group can also discuss the emotions that came up for them while doing this work. Some people might find that they are quite attached to their wealth and their control over it. For those individuals, the exercise provides an opportunity for discernment about detachment; for example, they might consider what it would look like if they wrote a new will with greater detachment from their wealth and possessions.

During the following week, participants will be invited to begin drafting new segments of their wills that reflect their new money rules. They will be crafting a narrative will, writing out what they want to say in their wills rather than drafting legal language.

Pentecost Week 4, Year A: Option 2 Forum and Exercise

The second option for the forum on Pentecost week 4 will build on the prior week's rule-crafting practice, but this week the rule-crafting will relate specifically to budgets. The rule-crafting matrix will be used to explore the possibility of a belief in creating a balanced budget. What are the changes in behavior that might enable a follower of Christ to have a balanced budget? Are there any unnecessary expenses? Could debts be consolidated?

	The Present	The Possibility
Behavior	Spend every paycheck.	
Belief	There is never enough.	Maintain a balanced budget.

As a result of this analysis, participants will be asked to consider new money rules that lead to a balanced budget. Once they complete this exercise, they will look toward developing the new money rules to achieve it.

	The Present	The Possibility
Behavior	Maintain a balanced budget.	
Belief	Maintain a balanced budget.	

How could this new money rule change their life? How might it affect their faith? Would it reduce their financial anxiety? For people who have suffered from economic discrimination, this exercise might be challenging. Economic injustice is a reason many people find themselves in financial distress. Rather than avoiding this topic, the exercise provides a chance to share the personal reasons people have struggled financially. This could be an opportunity for pastoral care and community support. It is also an opening for a congregational discussion of economic inequality and discrimination.

	The Present	The Possibility
Behavior	Maintain a balanced budget.	Financial confidence
Belief	Maintain a balanced budget.	Matt. 6:25–34

Again, this is a sensitive topic, and provisions must be made to protect privacy and confidentiality. In the trusting community of their local congregation, people might be able to discuss it. But if they are not able to trust their congregation, the leader will need to ask the group to consider another matrix. The forum participants might examine the distrust that exists in the congregation, which could be an additional reflection topic in their money memoirs. The goal of this exercise is not to develop balanced budgets for everyone, but for everyone to see that their faith can address finances and financial anxiety.

Pentecost Week 5, Year A: Sermon Plan

On Pentecost week 5, the appointed gospel is Matthew 11:16–19, 25–30. A sermon could focus on Matthew 11:30: "For my yoke is easy, and my burden is light." In addition, this week's scripture includes a challenging verse from Romans 7:19: "For I do not do the good I want, but the evil I do not want is what I do." Paul's epistle to the Romans sounds similar to psychotherapist Kate Levinson's descriptions of her clients' challenges with money. Levinson has found that most people feel shame regarding their financial affairs: some are ashamed of how much money they have, while others are ashamed of how they manage their money.[22] When it comes to money, many people find themselves doing the opposite of what they desire. After three weeks of challenging sermons and forums about money, the burden might not feel as light as Jesus suggests in the gospel. Therefore, this week's sermon could review how much ground the congregation has covered during this program. The congregation began by looking at the relationship between money and fear. Next, the program suggested alternative ways to use money. Finally, the people reflected on the social implications of their use of money and how they might use it in ways consistent with Christian theology. Through all of this, the congregation has been discussing the ways that money relates to gospel values. The sermon's goal is to demonstrate how the gospel's challenge of changing one's life, or at least one's relation to money, might be easier than it appears on the surface.

Pentecost Week 5, Year B: Option 1 Forum and Exercise

The first option for the forum on Pentecost week 5 will be led again by the wills and estate planning lawyer. Participants will be invited to share the changes they are making to their wills to reflect their new money rules. The lawyer might review the individual wills and changes. Creating a will is something concrete that people can do with their money, and the process can be empowering. People can gain a healthier perspective on money and perhaps reduce their attachment to it. As individuals start thinking about their money long term, they can also envision how their money will help them become more fully part of God's Beloved Community. By doing this work in a congregational setting, people can develop new congregational standards, which will help with the upcoming congregational ministry work in Year B.

---

22. Levinson, *Emotional Currency*, 27.

They can see what other believers are doing and how they are prioritizing gospel values in their wills. They can also hold each other accountable to those standards, making sure that their individual money rules are faithfully reflected in their estate planning and, ultimately, in their discipleship.

A final rule-crafting exercise will help reinforce the discernment process. It is an exercise that people can use whenever they are making a theological decision about money. The group can begin with the belief that their wills and money rules reflect their discipleship. That belief will help them determine whether their current behavior reflects that belief. If it does not, should they adopt new money rules?

	The Present	The Possibility
Behavior		Adopt new money rules.
Belief	My will/money rules reflect my faith.	

Underlying all this work is the belief in God's power to create all things new, including our relationship to money. In 2 Corinthians 5:17, Paul writes, "So if anyone is in Christ, there is a new creation: everything old has passed away; see, everything has become new!" What does this passage mean to the forum participants?

	The Present	The Possibility
Behavior		Adopt new money rules.
Belief	My will/money rules reflect my faith.	God makes all things new (2 Cor. 5:17).

This rule-crafting exercise provides a template for individual, congregational, and denominational conversations about money. As a result, an ongoing theological discussion about a Christian perspective on money can continue long after the completion of the curriculum.

Pentecost Week 5, Year A: Option 2 Forum and Exercise

The second forum for Pentecost week 5 will build on the work of the last three weeks, seeking to make a more explicitly theological connection. The group will contemplate the Trinity and a Trinitarian approach to personal spending and budgeting. The facilitator will provide a reminder overview of the concept of the Trinity as Creator, Redeemer, and Sustainer and as a community of three persons (Father, Son, and Holy Spirit) that live in perfect unity together. What would it mean for personal spending to be creative, redemptive, and sustaining? How might increased intentionality in spending choices truly support the entire community?

	The Present	The Possibility
Behavior		
Belief	Father, Son, and Holy Spirit	Creator, Redeemer, and Sustainer

Next, the group will examine whether their current belief in the Trinity affects their personal spending. Perhaps they are not connecting their purchases to the Trinity at all. What would it be like to do so? What would happen if they prioritized purchases that were creative, redemptive, and sustaining? For example, instead of buying groceries at a national grocery chain, perhaps they could make purchases at a local farmer's market; many local farmer's markets also support local artists and food banks.

	The Present	The Possibility
Behavior		Creative, redemptive, and sustaining purchases
Belief	Father, Son, and Holy Spirit	Creator, Redeemer, and Sustainer

The group could also consider the spending implications of considering the Trinity as a community. If God lives in the perfect community of the Father, Son, and Holy Spirit, what would it look like to prioritize purchases that reflect an anticompetitive community of all God's people? Where in their life and behavior is the Trinity present?

	The Present	The Possibility
Behavior		Farmer's market
Belief	Father, Son, and Holy Spirit	Community of three persons of God

As this program concludes, participants have the opportunity to continue to more actively align their faith and spending habits. Members might want to meet regularly so that they can work together to determine what are creative, redemptive, and sustaining purchases. They might also want to apply a Trinitarian lens to congregational and denominational spending. What would it look like for a parish and a diocese to spend money in ways that are creative, redemptive, and sustaining? Throughout the history of the church, Christians have been most successful at connecting their faith with their money when they have discussed money and possessions in community, and the same is likely to be true today. We read in the Acts of the Apostles and of monastic communities today and throughout the centuries who shared their resources, and those practices continue in intentional communities today. Through this discernment process, people can continually evaluate their budgets and their faith. In addition, these exercises can spark community discussion about money.

CHAPTER

7

Year B

Narrative Budgets and Investment Choices for Congregational Ministry

The pastoral plan for Year B includes four Sunday sermons and eight Sunday forums about money based on the scripture readings of the Revised Common Lectionary (RCL) for Pentecost weeks 2 through 5. There are two options for congregational forums and exercises. The first includes developing a narrative budget for the parish, often a popular and effective way to start a theological discussion of money within congregations. The second option focuses on the congregation's investment strategy, exploring the possibility of socially responsible investing. As with Year A, the focus is on the exercises rather than on the sermons or the forums, beyond their significance for explaining the exercises. Where Year A developed personal money rules, Year B helps the congregation develop its communal money rules. Again, as in Year A, the goal of these programs is to develop a comfort in discussing money that is essential to tackling the more challenging question of economic justice. By looking at parish budgets and investments, congregations can start to look at the role that their congregation can play in advancing justice and equity in their community and in the world.

Pentecost Week 2, Year B: Sermon Plan

On Pentecost week 2, the appointed gospel is Mark 2:23–3:6. A sermon could focus on Mark 2:27: "Then [Jesus] said to them, 'The sabbath was made for humankind, and not humankind for the sabbath.'" In this passage, Jesus critiqued the Pharisees' strict adherence to the letter, rather than the spirit, of the Mosaic law. Frequently, we do the same thing with money and budgets. Rather than looking at a budget as a tool for managing a family or an organization, it becomes a weapon that we use to obstruct constructive change. The Pharisees used the law to protect the status quo in this situation. Jesus contested their authority and ignored their legalistic interpretation of the law when he cured a man in 3:5: "He looked around at [the Pharisees] with anger; he was grieved at their hardness of heart and he said to the man, 'Stretch out your hand.' He stretched it out, and his hand was restored." Similarly, by challenging the ways our churches have traditionally thought about money and budgets, we can promote a kind of restoration in our congregations and in our communities.

During these weeks in Year B, we also read from 2 Corinthians 4:5–12. The Corinthian Christians were divided because of economic differences. Basically, the rich did not want to join with the poor. Yet Paul continually called them into being one body of Christ. This week's passage highlights the difficulty of discipleship but reaffirms the restorative power of Jesus's life and resurrection: "We are afflicted in every way, but not crushed; perplexed, but not driven to despair; persecuted, but not forsaken; struck down, but not destroyed; always carrying in the body the death of Jesus, so that the life of Jesus may also be made visible in our bodies" (4:8–10). Similarly, this week's sermon should highlight the restorative power of Jesus in every aspect of our lives, including our individual wealth and our congregational assets.

Pentecost Week 2, Year B: Option 1 Forum and Exercise

The first option for a forum during Pentecost week 2 focuses on the fundamentals of narrative budgeting. The congregation's treasurer could hand out copies of the current budget, and the rector (or another member of the staff or vestry) could describe a narrative budget process, which clarifies the financial priorities of the congregation through discussion and discernment before developing a spreadsheet. For example, when determining the budget for the building and grounds, the congregation would take into account the external organizations that use its facilities alongside parish groups, considering their various impacts on the buildings. A narrative budget clarifies how all funds are used and why they matter to the church's ministry and the gospel. Budgets are an excellent way to start a relatively objective conversation about money. From the beginning, the rector should make it clear that the goal of this program is not to draft a definitive budget but to develop congregational money habits and rules.

After explaining the goals of a narrative budget, the rector (or another individual) leads the group in a conversation about spending priorities:

1. What are the top spending priorities for the upcoming year?
2. What are new spending priorities for the upcoming year?
3. What programs or activities might be reduced or eliminated?
4. What emotions come up for you during this conversation?
5. What Bible stories or teachings of Jesus seem relevant?

During the upcoming week, parishioners will again be encouraged to use their money memoirs to reflect on the congregation's use of money and its potential money rules.

Pentecost Week 2, Year B: Option 2 Forum and Exercise

The second option for a forum during Pentecost week 2 focuses on the fundamentals of socially responsible investing. The congregation's treasurer (or investment committee chair) might hand out copies of the church's current balance sheet and investment portfolio before providing a quick overview. Then an investment advisor or a member of the church's investment committee would describe the church's current investment strategy.

The investment advisor would also outline the basics of socially responsible investing. Generally, socially responsible investing determines which investments should be excluded from a portfolio, how much oversight the investors would like to have over the companies in which they invest, and the community impact of their investments.[1]

1. Are there products or services in which the congregation does not want to invest?
2. How much oversight does the congregation want to exercise over their investments? Are congregants willing to monitor the companies' decisions and raise objections at the annual meeting?
3. Are there community investments that the congregation would like to make that could have an impact locally?

During the upcoming week, participants will again be encouraged to use their money memoirs to reflect on the congregation's investments and potential money rules.

Pentecost Week 3, Year B: Sermon Plan

For Pentecost week 3, the appointed gospel is Mark 3:20–35. In this passage, the Scribes and Jesus's own family questioned whether

1. Murphy, ed., *Faithful Investing*, 12.

he was possessed by Beelzebub, because he healed a man on the Sabbath. Jesus argued that he is in right relationship with God, because if he were Satan, then how could he cast out Satan (Mark 3:23)? Jesus emphasized the importance of right relationship with God. We, as followers of Christ, are called into right relationship with God and so, too, are the choices we make with our money. Are we consumed by a prideful relation to our money, or do we have a healthy detachment from it? Jesus demonstrated that he has control over Satan rather than the other way around. What about us? Does our money control us, or do we control our money? This question applies not only to individuals but also to congregations. Is our budget controlling our ministry, or is our ministry driving our budget?

This week's passage from 2 Corinthians also tests our assumptions about money. Paul writes, "So we are ambassadors for Christ, since God is making his appeal through us; we entreat you on behalf of Christ, be reconciled to God" (5:20). As "ambassadors for Christ" are we using our individual and congregational resources in ways that reflect Christ's ministry? Are we missing an opportunity to reconcile our wealth to God? This week's sermon aims to blend individual and congregational money rules.

Pentecost Week 3, Year B: Option 1 Forum and Exercise

The first option for the forum during Pentecost week 3 focuses on the congregation's budget priorities from the prior week. However, this week evaluates zero-based budgeting (ZBB) as a means for determining priorities. In ZBB, every line item on the budget starts at zero and requires an explanation and justification for spending anything on that line item during the upcoming year. After members of the staff and vestry explain the proposed budget, the congregation works through the following steps:

1. List each of the ministries and programs that will be reviewed, along with current spending.
2. For each ministry, a presenter leads a group discussion of the question, "If we were not already doing this work, knowing what we now know, would we begin it—and would we do it the same way?"
3. After the ministry discussion, the congregation lists the anticipated costs (and any potential income) for each ministry and program.
4. Finally, all congregants evaluate whether specific programs, functions, or activities should be eliminated or modified.[2]

At the end of this session, participants might consider the following questions:

1. What emotions came up for you during this conversation?
2. What Bible stories or teachings of Jesus seem relevant?

During this forum, the rector or another leader might introduce the concept of idolatry and congregational ministry. Is there an "idol" in the church's budget? What things are consuming the majority of the congregation's resources? Do they reflect everything that the congregation would like to be? Do they reflect a distant memory or an unrealistic hope? Sometimes, for a congregation to grow, it must first prune. It might need to eliminate programs or fixtures from the past that will not contribute to their future. More importantly, is there a program or fixture that is inhibiting the congregation's ability to address economic injustice? This can be a difficult conversation but one that might be necessary for the parish to flourish. At the end of the session, participants are again invited to use their money memoirs during the upcoming week to reflect on

2. Murray Dropkin, Jim Halpin, and Bill La Touche, *The Budget-Building Book for Nonprofits: A Step-by-Step Guide for Managers and Boards* (San Francisco: John Wiley & Sons, 2007), 32.

the congregation's use of money and what new money rules reflect the congregation's priorities and vision.

Pentecost Week 3: Year B, Option 2 Forum and Exercise

The second option for the forum during Pentecost week 3 discusses the investment priorities identified the prior week. However, this week, the group will use Jane Patterson and Steven Tomlinson's rule-crafting matrix. The conversation might start by questioning the belief that the congregation must earn the best return on its investments. Many vestries and investment committees believe that their fiduciary duty requires securing the best possible returns for the congregation. Presumably, that belief would be reflected in the congregation's current investment portfolio.

	The Present	The Possibility
Behavior	Current portfolio	
Belief	Get the best return on investment.	

This exercise empowers participants to consider a different belief. What if the congregation tried to earn a good return from socially responsible investing? Would it have to sacrifice investment performance? Not necessarily. According to KLD Indexes, from 2009 to 2019 the annualized returns for socially responsible investment funds was 10.63 percent, compared to 10.17 percent for the S&P 500.[3] Those results are likely to be even better when

3. Shauna Carther Heyford, "Socially Responsible Mutual Funds," *Investopedia*, June 25, 2019, accessed September 9, 2020, *https://www.investopedia.com/articles/mutualfund/03/030503.asp.*

technology stocks outperform the market, because socially responsible funds tend to focus heavily on high-technology stocks. Technology companies generally have a low environmental impact and strong wages and benefits for employees, which makes them popular investments for socially responsible investors.

	The Present	The Possibility
Behavior	Current portfolio	Add socially responsible funds.
Belief	Get the best return on investment.	Get a socially responsible return.

If the congregation prioritizes socially responsible investing, it will begin to adopt a new money rule: invest in socially responsible mutual funds.

Again, during the week participants will be encouraged to write in their money memoirs about the experience of considering this communal money rule, and they will be challenged to reflect on what socially responsible investing might mean for their own investing.

Pentecost Week 4, Year B: Sermon Plan

For Pentecost week 4, the appointed gospel is Mark 4:26–34. In this passage, Jesus used the image of the tiny mustard seed that "becomes the greatest of all shrubs, and puts forth large branches, so that the birds of the air can make nests in its shade" (Mark 4:32). This parable is a wonderful illustration of God's abundance. From something so small can grow a huge tree that supports new life. It also suggests that Christians might approach money with joy rather than dread, because it can be a source of creation. Money can support all sorts of new life, in individuals and in the church. Similarly, congregational money can support new worship, new parish life, and new outreach.

This week's passage from 2 Corinthians also highlights the theme of God's abundance. In 2 Corinthians 5:17, Paul declared, "So if anyone is in Christ, there is a new creation: everything old has passed away; see, everything has become new!" What could become new for this congregation as it examines its budget and tells the story of its common life? What are new money rules the congregation could embrace?

Pentecost Week 4, Year B: Option 1 Forum and Exercise

The first forum for Pentecost week 4 will clarify the congregation's budget priorities. This session will use the rule-crafting matrix and starts with the belief that the congregation must have a balanced budget.

	The Present	The Possibility
Behavior		
Belief	Must have balanced budget.	

That belief, however, might be limiting the congregation's ability to worship and conduct outreach, because a balanced budget might require ongoing reductions in expenses and staff time.

	The Present	The Possibility
Behavior	Cutting expenses, staff time	
Belief	Must have balanced budget.	God's abundance, parable of the mustard seed

If the congregation truly embraced God's abundance, as reflected in the parable of the mustard seed, it might look differently at stewardship and other sources of revenue. In that case, the congregation might develop a new money rule dedicated to personal stewardship and innovative congregational fundraising.

	The Present	The Possibility
Behavior	Cutting expenses, staff time	New fundraising efforts
Belief	Must have balanced budget.	God's abundance, feeding 5,000

This exercise illustrates how a congregation might discern its new money habits and rules. A congregation will not necessarily adopt all these rules, but this exercise introduces a practice the congregation can use going forward. Furthermore, by establishing those rules in community, the congregation is far more likely to adhere to and hold each other accountable to them, just as the early Christian communities described in the Acts of the Apostles and the Benedictines in their Rule of Life.

Pentecost Week 4, Year B: Option 2 Forum and Exercise

The second forum for Pentecost week 4 introduces a different type of socially responsible investing: impact investing. What would it look like if the congregation made investments designed to have an impact on a local community? Instead of simply investing in socially responsible mutual funds, it might also consider local impact investments such as microlending programs, which make small loans to local low-income entrepreneurs. Microfinance was pioneered by Muhammad Yunus at Grameen Bank in Bangladesh to develop a credit delivery program for the rural poor, and it has been amazingly successful. Microfinance has not been as successful in the United States because credit is more readily available. Nevertheless, these programs can be transformative for people. Instead of focusing exclusively on securing the best returns for its investments, the congregation might also experiment with opportunities for impact investing within its community and more widely.

	The Present	The Possibility
Behavior	Current portfolio	
Belief	Get the best return on investment.	Get an impactful return on investment.

If the congregation agrees to prioritize an impactful return, it could begin to modify its investing behavior. Further, impact investments offer the congregation another link to the larger community, support to its outreach ministries, and a way for the congregation to directly address economic inequality through its investments. The metrics around the success of impact investments will not look the same as typical investing. These investments will not yield market rates of return, but frequently they will yield better returns than savings accounts or certificates of deposit (CDs).

Pentecost Week 5, Year B: Sermon Plan

For Pentecost week 5, the appointed epistle is 2 Corinthians 6:1–13. Paul wrote of the many hardships that he and the early Christians endured because of the grace of God: "We are treated as imposters, and yet are true; as unknown, and yet are well known; as dying, and see—we are alive; as punished, and yet not killed; as sorrowful, yet always rejoicing; as poor, yet making many rich; as having nothing, and yet possessing everything" (6:8–10). What might it mean for a congregation to view itself as "possessing everything"?

This week's appointed gospel is Mark 4:35–41, a passage in which Jesus calmed the sea and subsequently asked the disciples why they had been so frightened by the storm. As described in chapter 1, money matters, including making changes to budgets and questioning financial priorities, can evoke fear and anxiety in any system, particularly within a congregation. Therefore, this week's sermon should offer calm and hope in the midst of change. It could remind congregants that faith enables us to confront change and remain hopeful because of the knowledge of God's love and grace.

Pentecost Week 5, Year B: Option 1 Forum and Exercise

The first forum for Pentecost week 5 combines the work of the last three weeks. Based on its money rules, how might the congregation shift its budgetary priorities? Individuals will be invited to share the congregational money rules that they discerned after the prior week's sessions. Are their new rules founded on a scriptural or theological basis? For example, what would it mean to sincerely believe Paul's radical claim of Christians "possessing everything"?

	The Present	The Possibility
Behavior		
Belief		"possessing everything" (2 Cor. 6:10)

Could that belief inspire a change in behavior? Perhaps, if the congregation embraced 2 Corinthians 6:10, there might be less anxiety about the budget. How might that sense of liberation change the habits and rules of the congregation?

	The Present	The Possibility
Behavior		Less anxiety about budget
Belief		"possessing everything" (2 Cor. 6:10)

Perhaps a congregation would become more confident in its financial position and more willing to take financial risk in order to advance justice and equity. For example, a new money rule might be to set aside 10 percent of the budget for new projects or ministries that are not identified when the budget was approved. After completing this rule-crafting exercise, the congregation can discern how to modify its budget or fundraising expectations as it adopts new money rules. Finally, the participants might be asked how to make the budget a reality. While these rule-crafting exercises are applied to congregational money rules in this program, they can also be applied to personal money rules. Describing these rules in a congregational setting might facilitate people's understanding, and it might minimize the prospect of individuals becoming defensive when considering their own money rules.

Pentecost Week 5, Year B: Option 2 Forum and Exercise

The second forum for Pentecost week 5 will build on the work of the last three weeks, making a more explicitly theological connection. The group discussion will center on the Trinity and what a Trinitarian investment strategy would look like. The facilitator might want to provide a brief overview of the concept of the Trinity as Creator, Redeemer, and Sustainer. What if the congregation sought investments that were creative, redemptive, and sustaining? The participants will also evaluate investments that truly support the entire community. In the same way that the three persons of the Trinity support each other in noncompetitive ways, how could the congregation select investments that support the entire community, not just the congregation? Could the congregation prioritize investments that support the local community and still provide some level of return? Using the rule-crafting matrix, the group starts by examining their current belief in the Trinity and the possibility of envisioning the Trinity as Creator, Redeemer, and Sustainer.

	The Present	The Possibility
Behavior		
Belief	Father, Son, and Holy Spirit	Creator, Redeemer, and Sustainer

Next, the group might consider whether their current belief in the Trinity affects the congregation's investment strategy. Perhaps the congregation is deferring to investment advisors in the same way that Christians sometimes defer to an understanding of God the Father. Sometimes, Christians forget that all three persons of the Trinity (Father, Son, and Holy Spirit) are coequal. What would happen if the congregation prioritized investments that were creative, redemptive, and sustaining at the same time?

	The Present	The Possibility
Behavior	Defer to authority.	
Belief	Father, Son, and Holy Spirit	Creator, Redeemer, and Sustainer

The group could also reflect on the investment implications of understanding the Trinity to be a community. If God lives in perfect noncompetitive community of the Father, Son, and Holy Spirit, what would it look like for congregational investments to reflect a harmonious community of all God's people? Perhaps a communal view of the Trinity reveals the need for the congregation to try impact investing that benefits the entire community and not just the investor. The Trinity also reminds Christians that Jesus is the antirival; he is the one who represents the exact opposite of human rivalry. Perhaps the congregation's investment strategy should not be based on comparisons to other organizations' rates of return but rather on the congregation's mission.

	The Present	The Possibility
Behavior	Defer to authority.	Community, impact investments
Belief	Father, Son, and Holy Spirit	Community of three persons of God

As this program concludes, the congregation should have the opportunity to play a more active role in its investments. In particular, it might want to set aside a portion of its portfolio for impactful community investments. For example, local small businesses might need investors. The Israelites believed that debt forgiveness was a form of redemption; perhaps there are debts that the congregation can forgive. Similarly, many congregations inside and outside of the Episcopal Church have been using their resources to buy and forgive medical debt. Medical debt can be purchased and forgiven at a fraction of its face value, which makes for a highly effective investment. Putting faith into action through targeted investments is a good way to continue a theological discussion of money and to move closer to becoming God's Beloved Community.

CHAPTER

8

Year C

Resource Sharing and Advocacy for Global Mission

The pastoral plan for Year C includes four Sunday sermons and eight Sunday forums about money and liberation theology based on the scripture readings of the Revised Common Lectionary (RCL) for Easter weeks 3 through 6. As with the pastoral plans in the previous chapters, the primary focus is on the exercises that engage a theological discussion of money. In many ways, Year C is a culmination of the prior two years. After developing a familiarity with discussing money in personal and congregational contexts, Year C provides a global context and addresses economic justice more directly than in Years A and B. For Year C, the first option will discuss offering support to economically disadvantaged congregations within a diocese. The second option will evaluate providing economic support for churches within the Anglican Communion. How might participants consider the economic system of the Episcopal Church and the Anglican Communion in an attempt to develop globally contextual money rules?

Easter Week 3, Year C: Sermon Plan

On Easter week 3 of Year C, Revelation 5:12 is one of the assigned scripture verses: "Worthy is the Lamb that was slaughtered to receive power and wealth and wisdom and might and honor and glory and blessing!" This passage exemplifies the sacrificial logic that appears in many theologies of salvation, and it provides an opportunity for a sermon addressing the shortcomings of sacrificial thinking.[1] Sacrificial thinking proposes that some people are required to sacrifice for the benefit of others, and it is typically justified by Jesus's crucifixion. This thinking stems from early Christian thinkers who pointed to Isaiah 53:1–12 as a prophecy regarding Christ's coming and his sacrificial death. The importance of Christ's sacrifice is further reinforced throughout the New Testament. Many prominent Christian theologians, including Augustine of Hippo, Anselm of Canterbury, and Thomas Aquinas, have argued for the importance of sacrifice in Christianity. Sacrificial thinking is deeply rooted in substitutionary atonement theory, which holds that Jesus had to die to absolve the sins of humanity.

A similar type of thinking has worked its way into the church's understanding of money. Christians frequently view money from a standpoint of sacrifice and scarcity, overlooking the themes of God's abundance.[2] While individual sacrifice can have some tremendous benefits, liberation theologian Jung Mo Sung admonishes Christians to move beyond sacrificial thinking, arguing that it perpetuates and justifies systemic economic inequality. Sacrifice has also become an accepted part of economic thinking. To foster economic growth and progress, economists have argued that sacrifices are necessary during economic recessions, even though those sacrifices disproportionately affect the poor while benefiting the rich.[3] The unequal

1. Jung Mo Sung, *Desire, Market, Religion* (London: SCM Press, 2007), 98.
2. Brueggemann, *Money and Possessions*, 22–23.
3. Sung, *Desire, Market, Religion*, 18.

outcome of the economic cycle is generally accepted as a market reality, which has led Sung to conclude that most people believe that sacrifice is normal. Furthermore, sacrifice is either required to make one's way to heaven or to overcome one's sins, including the sin of being poor.[4]

While Jesus never declared poverty to be a sin, the current consumerist capitalist culture views poverty as a sin and wealth a virtue. It declares the wealthy to be winners and the poor as losers who only have themselves to blame for their poverty. To overcome abusive sacrificial thinking, we need to reject its perversions. Sung argues that Christians can overcome sacrificial thinking by returning to the transcendence of God. God has created the economic markets, and God reigns over the markets, not the converse. This is not to suggest replacing market idolatry with a transcendent God who permits noneconomic forms of inequity. Instead, our faith is in a relational and unitive God. With an understanding of God as One with whom we have a relationship rather than a God that stands apart, then relatedness with God includes and incorporates relatedness with other people. This relatedness to God and to others raises questions about personal money habits and the inequity that exists in the world's current money habits. New global money habits and rules that reflect the gospel values are needed.

Easter Week 3, Year C: Option 1 Forum and Exercise

While Year A discussed personal money rules and Year B discussed congregational money rules, Year C focuses on a global perspective. The global economic market has taken on religious undertones in North America, with a form of sacrificial thinking justifying the North American bias that the wealthy have made the right sacrifices to earn their success. Conversely, it implies that those without

4. Sung, *Desire, Market, Religion*, 19.

wealth have not sacrificed enough. This approach to money leaves little room for luck, inheritance, systemic inequity, or God's grace. Rather, all success is attributed to the market and the individual, a belief that represents the idolatry of the market and the individual.[5] This perspective also reinforces a bias, deeply rooted in Western culture, that people are poor because they are lazy. In the Old Testament, Pharaoh used similar logic when he insisted that the Israelites work even harder while enslaved in Egypt (Exod. 5:15–17).[6] Sacrificial thinking develops when people disregard Jesus's commandment to love one another. To help the discernment process, the group might want to develop new global money rules taking into account the Baptismal Covenant through the lens of the rule-crafting practice. In the Episcopal Church, we regularly reaffirm the Baptismal Covenant. But how often do we contemplate what it means in a global setting? If we agree to "respect the dignity of every human being," how does that affirmation materialize in our behavior and our beliefs? Should our behavior change?[7]

	The Present	The Possibility
Behavior	Recite Baptismal Covenant regularly.	
Belief	"Respect the dignity of every human being."	

In considering the possibility, we might envision a global commitment to love and care for others. Out of this discernment, new money rules might appear. For example, the congregation might

5. Sung, *Desire, Market, Religion*, 69, 72.

6. Zabriskie, ed., *Social Justice Bible Challenge*, 22–23.

7. *Book of Common Prayer*, 305.

commit a percentage of its budget to support another congregation in its diocese or in the Anglican Communion.

	The Present	The Possibility
Behavior	Recite Baptismal Covenant regularly.	Share congregational assets.
Belief	"Respect the dignity of every human being."	Love all human beings.

Easter Week 3, Year C: Option 2 Forum and Exercise

The second forum for Easter week 3 begins a conversation about global money rules with a focus on the Anglican Communion. In the Episcopal Church, every church operates independently, unless it is a diocesan-funded mission. Of course, churches pay their diocesan apportionments and dioceses pay national apportionments, but most Episcopal churches make fairly independent budget decisions and derive their income independently. Similarly, in the Anglican Communion, each province operates more or less independently. The sacrificial thinking described earlier might color our Western perceptions of some of the provinces, especially those that are former British or American colonies. This reinforces a bias that certain churches lack resources because their members and leaders are lazy or incompetent. However, Hosea 6:4–6 and Matthew 9:13 prioritize justice and mercy over sacrifice. The group should be encouraged to consider what justice and mercy might look like in other parts of the Anglican Communion. Does the economic inequality in the Anglican Communion demand a response from congregations in the Episcopal Church? How might the rule-crafting process focused through the Baptismal Covenant apply to the full Anglican Communion and a global commitment to love and care for others?

	The Present	The Possibility
Behavior	Recite Baptismal Covenant regularly.	
Belief	"Respect the dignity of every human being."	

Perhaps the parish could make a commitment to support churches that extend beyond the Episcopal Church within the Anglican Communion. The relationship should be reciprocal in some way rather than one church simply writing a check to another church. The churches could facilitate an exchange or begin to develop a relationship via video. In this way, they would start to embody the Beloved Community.

	The Present	The Possibility
Behavior	Recite Baptismal Covenant regularly.	Sister parish
Belief	"Respect the dignity of every human being."	Love all human beings.

Ultimately, the goal is for the group to discern collectively how it might effectively allocate its money and resources to express its discipleship and faith in a global context.

Easter Week 4, Year C: Sermon Plan

On Easter week 4 of Year C, Psalm 23:1 is one of the assigned scripture verses. In it, the psalmist acknowledged human desire when he declared, "The Lord is my shepherd, I shall not want." But human desire can perpetuate inequality. Christians, therefore, need to discern carefully the role of desire in their lives and in their discipleship. Theologian Eve Poole acknowledges that desire comes from God and argues that we ought not to resist desire entirely, but to curb it toward God. The Old Testament writers were well aware of the insatiability of human desire when they committed themselves to the tenth commandment against coveting the possessions of others.

Human desire remains a mystery to most people. We have a limited ability to mitigate its destructive power alone, which makes it an important sermon topic. Desire emerges from a complex mix of biology, culture, and norms, which makes it difficult to understand on our own,[8] but biblical passages like Psalm 23 suggest that God calls us to transcend our base desires while recognizing those desires are God-given. Our goal might be not to deny our desires but to strive to bend them toward justice for all and toward the divine. Together, congregations can confront the complexity of desire and the ways it manifests in individual, congregational, and global money habits and rules.

Easter Week 4, Year C: Option 1 Forum and Exercise

The first forum for Easter week 4 will provide more background on desire and inequality. There will also be an overview of the economic inequality that has developed under our consumerist capitalistic system. This inequality exists within the Episcopal Church. Some churches have large endowments, and others have no assets with no overarching obligation to share resources. Economic inequality extends to the entire Anglican Communion as well. In response, liberation theologian Ignacio Ellacuría calls for a change to culture; he calls on us to challenge the assumptions and desires of our culture.

8. Ivone Gebara, *Longing for Running Water: Ecofeminism and Liberation* (Minneapolis: Fortress Press, 1999), 206.

We can start with a change in culture within the Episcopal Church by questioning our monetary practices. Should vast income inequality exist between Episcopal congregations? Or should the Episcopal Church provide a different model from that of the world? Can we be an institution that downplays competition, envy, and rivalry, focusing instead on community and sharing? When discussing culture, it is typical for North Americans to focus on the dominant cultures of that location. But liberation theologians like Sung and Ellacuría urge North Americans to focus on the people on the margins. What might a theological discussion of money in the Episcopal Church look like if it were led by members who live on the margins of the dominant culture or outside the boundaries of the United States? In addition, Ellacuría notes that both the oppressed and the oppressor are hurt under the current economic system.[9] While the rich might have a surfeit of possessions, materialism also impairs those people, albeit in emotional and spiritual ways. The rampant desire for material things spurs financial anxiety.[10]

Prayerfully discerning the difference between desire and need is a critical step toward understanding our relationship with money and resolving global inequality. The following rule-crafting exercise examines the difference between desire and need. The exercise could start with the belief that individuals in the United States do not have all that they need. While many people might not readily admit to the fear underlying that belief, North American behavior in general reveals the prevalence of that belief. As a result, people hoard goods and take all means necessary to protect themselves. In response, the group could consider the disposition of trust envisioned by Jesus in Matthew 6:25–26:

---

9. Ignacio Ellacuría, *Ignacio Ellacuría: Essays on History, Liberation, and Salvation*, ed. Michael E. Lee (Maryknoll, NY: Orbis Books, 2013), 184.

10. Sung, *Desire, Market, Religion*, 34.

Therefore I tell you, do not worry about your life, what you will eat or what you will drink, or about your body, what you will wear. Is not life more than food, and the body more than clothing? Look at the birds of the air; they neither sow nor reap nor gather into barns, and yet your heavenly Father feeds them. Are you not of more value than they?

	The Present	The Possibility
Behavior	Planning, hoarding, anxiety	
Belief	I do not have all that I need.	"Do not worry about your life" (Matt. 6:25–26).

If people embraced Jesus's teaching in Matthew 6, how might their spending behaviors change, and how might their individual, congregational, and global money rules change? Perhaps they would hear the gospel calling them and their congregation to share more of their resources.

	The Present	The Possibility
Behavior	Planning, hoarding, anxiety	Share more resources.
Belief	I do not have all that I need.	"Do not worry about your life" (Matt. 6:25–26).

This exercise also naturally leads to a discussion about inequality within the Anglican Communion. How might congregations share their resources with other churches and other people in need within the Anglican Communion? The following exercise will help the group discern new money rules addressing global inequality. The exercise might also challenge the belief that congregations should operate independently, which could empower members to worry less about their budgets and their assets as they shift their focus to others.

	The Present	The Possibility
Behavior	Congregations worry about their own finances.	
Belief	Congregations operate independently.	

After a discussion of the economic disparities in the Anglican Communion, participants might consider a change in behavior. In particular, they might feel called to explore the implications of truly being one body of Christ. If each individual and congregation is part of the body of Christ and each has different talents and gifts, how might this congregation be called to share their assets more fully?

	The Present	The Possibility
Behavior	Congregations worry about their own finances.	Congregations pool assets.
Belief	Congregations operate independently.	Body of Christ

If the congregation agrees that it could adopt a new money habit by sharing more of its assets, it might start to evaluate its budget to determine how it could support other congregations. Furthermore, careful discernment regarding an approach to sharing resources can be part of an ongoing congregational project and theological discussion of money. Ultimately, a congregation could model noncompetitive sharing for others.

Easter Week 4, Year C: Option 2 Forum and Exercise

The second forum for Easter week 4 will focus on the perils of desire and global inequality. Mimetic desire is growing exponentially as the world becomes more connected and we see what others have. This rapid expansion of mimetic desire is helping preserve the current inequality in the world. Using the rule-crafting matrix, the group could discuss mimetic desire. The conversation starts with current behavior, in which people generally work to preserve the status quo, then explore the belief that people need what others have.

	The Present	The Possibility
Behavior	Buy and keep status quo.	
Belief	I need what others have.	"A fair portion of the riches of this land" (826).

The rule-crafting exercise could explore alternative beliefs. What could be a competing belief to counter mimetic desire? In the Prayer for the Oppressed in the Book of Common Prayer, we pray that God "grant that every one of us may enjoy a fair portion of the riches of this land."[11] What constitutes a fair portion? This conversation could lead participants to consider the value of sufficiency and to set the standards for what constitutes a "fair portion,"

11. *Book of Common Prayer*, 826.

as in the Acts of the Apostles and monastic orders. This discernment process can establish community standards, and it can help individuals discern their own standards in a global context.

Easter Week 5, Year C: Sermon Plan

On Easter week 5 of Year C, John 13:34 is an assigned scripture: "I give you a new commandment, that you love one another. Just as I have loved you, you also should love one another." With Jesus's commandment, this week's sermon can move from a critique of existing systems to the creation of new systems that help build God's Beloved Community. For instance, the new system might be one in which congregations do not only look out for themselves but for other congregations as well.

The divine ideal of loving one another is memorialized in the Eucharist and enlivened in the Trinity. Thus, they offer liturgical models of economic justice. In the Eucharist, all share the same bread and wine. There is enough for everyone and everyone receives the same, so there is no opportunity for mimetic desire. The example of the Eucharist might be an effective way to engage listeners around the importance of inclusion and equality among the people of God. It might also provide another opening to engage congregations in discerning how they might share their recourses. Preachers can also point to the Eucharist to demonstrate the prevalence of inequality, even in worship. The bread and wine that become the body and blood of Christ are generally produced by an economic system that relies on unfair agricultural practices and wage inequality.[12] Leaders might focus on liberation theologian Enrique Dussel's call for Christians to condemn the current global system and envision a more equitable system, in the same way that Jesus challenged

---

12. Enrique Dussel, *Beyond Liberation: Ethics, History, Marxism, and Liberation Theology*, ed. Eduardo Mendieta (Lanham, MD: Rowman & Littlefield, 2003), 43, 50.

the Roman Empire and the Jewish temple system.[13] One practical way to engage in this kind of work is to reconsider how congregations support themselves financially.

Easter Week 5, Year C: Option 1 Forum and Exercise

The first forum for Easter week 5 will focus on the Trinity. Liberationist theologians Leonardo and Clodovis Boff point out that the Trinity provides a model of a "unified society of equals."[14] In the Trinity, the three persons of God live in "perfect communion," providing a "prototype for what society should be. . . . By affirming and respecting personal individuality, it should enable persons to live in such communion and collaboration with each other."[15] By envisioning our congregations as embodiments of the Trinity, a Sunday forum could inspire congregants to think differently about global money rules. A facilitator could pose questions about the Trinity and its economic implications: If God is equal in all three persons of the Trinity, is economic inequality consistent with the Trinity? If there are no greater or lesser persons of the Trinity, why would God endorse an economic system that makes some greater and some lesser than others, or a system that requires some, but not others, to sacrifice?

Again, the forum returns to the rule-crafting exercise of the prior weeks and a consideration of the Trinity. Whether as Father, Son, and Holy Spirit or as Creator, Redeemer, and Sustainer, these words do not fundamentally change belief in the Trinity, yet they shift the focus, which could provoke changes in behavior. The rule-crafting exercise can help participants reconsider the full implications of the Trinity and to develop new money rules.

---

13. Dussel, *Beyond Liberation*, 153.

14. Leonardo Boff and Clodovis Boff, *Introducing Liberation Theology*, trans. Paul Burns (Maryknoll, NY: Orbis Books, 2016), 52.

15. Boff and Boff, *Introducing Liberation Theology*, 52.

	The Present	The Possibility
Behavior		
Belief	Father, Son, and Holy Spirit	Creator, Redeemer, and Sustainer

What behavior results from belief in the Trinity as Father, Son, and Holy Spirt, and what behavior might result from envisioning the Trinity as Creator, Redeemer, and Sustainer? For example, maybe people only consider the Trinity when they are making the sign of the cross, but perhaps the Trinity could be impactful for them in other dimensions of their life and faith. In thinking about the Trinity as Creator, Redeemer, and Sustainer, people might prioritize spending of time and money that is creative, redemptive, and sustaining. The group would benefit from further discussion to determine what makes a purchase or choice creative, redemptive, and sustaining. This process might ultimately serve as a tool for setting community standards.

	The Present	The Possibility
Behavior	Make the sign of the cross.	Purchase in accord with Trinity.
Belief	Father, Son, and Holy Spirit	Creator, Redeemer, and Sustainer

Some Christians object to characterizing the Trinity as Creator, Redeemer, and Sustainer. Some believers fear that such a characterization would reduce the Trinity to modalism, which focuses on the three persons of the Trinity individually and overlooks the mystery of their unity. However, even critics acknowledge that this new language can supplement the traditional understanding of the Trinity,[16] perhaps enabling a broader and more comprehensive view of life in God.

Easter Week 5, Year C: Option 2 Forum and Exercise

The second forum for Easter week 5 will also discuss the Trinity as a model of a "unified society of equals."[17] Where the first option evaluated individual purchasing, the second option will address a more global focus, asking participants what the global economy would look like if it embodied the Trinitarian framework of a society of equals.

	The Present	The Possibility
Behavior		
Belief	Father, Son, and Holy Spirit	Unified society of equals

If Christians truly acted as a unified society of equals, how might the global economy change? Would people continue to support the status quo so reflexively?

	The Present	The Possibility
Behavior	Support status quo.	
Belief	Father, Son, and Holy Spirit	Unified society of equals

16. Cunningham, *These Three Are One*, 70–71.

17. Boff and Boff, *Introducing Liberation Theology*, 52.

Discussing what it means to have an economy that honors a "unified society of equals" could produce fruitful insights, and it might serve to aggregate the reflections from earlier exercises. Based on these earlier exercises, the group might be able to discern community standards. They might be able to agree on a number of universal basic rights and privileges for all God's children. Ultimately, this discernment work could produce a congregational project that continues long after the end of this program.

Easter Week 6, Year C: Sermon Plan

In Easter week 6 of Year C, John 14:27 is one of the assigned scripture verses. In his farewell address, Jesus said, "Peace I leave with you; my peace I give you. I do not give to you as the world gives. Do not let your hearts be troubled, and do not let them be afraid." Jesus encouraged his disciples to act on his message and not to let fear keep them from it. Christians are called to bring Jesus's message to a world that has too often fallen prey to false idols and sacrifice. After clarifying the Christian commitment to equality, preachers will need to lead the congregation to consider what they can do next, recognizing there is not one common goal for all congregations. The final sermon on this topic should convey a sense of urgency. The statistics overwhelmingly demonstrate that inequality is increasing and accelerating around the world, so the sermon must incorporate a call to action.[18] Ellacuría argues that one cannot wait to be concerned with the poor until after one has become wealthy and secure; Christians must address poverty and inequality now.[19] They need a healthy sense of outrage over

18. Matt Egan, "Record Inequality," CNN Business, September 27, 2017, accessed November 4, 2017, *http://money.cnn.com/2017/09/27/news/economy/inequality-record-top-1-percent-wealth/index.html.*

19. Ellacuría, *Essays on History, Liberation, and Salvation*, 246.

injustice.[20] If the prior sermons and discussions have been successful, people should already have some sense of urgency. The call to action will be reinforced in the Sunday forum.

Easter Week 6, Year C: Option 1 Forum and Exercise

The first forum for Easter week 6 will focus on identifying a congregational project that addresses global inequality. The goal is for the congregation to choose a group project that addresses some of the issues surrounding money that were raised during this pastoral program.[21] A discussion group might explore various options for global action. Facilitators might need to remind congregants that cultural change is a critical prerequisite to any political or economic change. When we start to change our own behavior, we incrementally alter our attitudes and "rewire our brains," which will be a necessary first step toward becoming God's Beloved Community.[22] So, congregants might consider how they can affect a cultural change that addresses inequality. To discern a congregational project, it might help to return to the possibility of new global money rules. Perhaps the congregation can start with the ideal of loving our neighbor as ourselves, and it could advocate for neighbors with fewer economic resources. For example, the congregation could provide financial assistance to another congregation. It could also develop a program of financial education or advocate for banning inequitable financial instruments such as payday loans, which disadvantage low-income individuals.

20. Ivan Petrella, *Beyond Liberation Theology: A Polemic* (London: SCM Press, 2008), 124.

21. Ellacuría, *Essays on History, Liberation, and Salvation*, 114, 235, 277.

22. Poole, *Buying* God, 103.

	The Present	The Possibility
Behavior		Advocate for your neighbor.
Belief		Love your neighbor as yourself.

To reach these goals, a congregation must candidly discuss and acknowledge its current behavior and beliefs. While many individuals might want to make a change, the change can be difficult. Such changes are adaptive to the congregation, and they are generally met with resistance. In addition, all will need to recognize that social transformation is not a static event but an ongoing process.

	The Present	The Possibility
Behavior	Protect the status quo.	Advocate for your neighbor.
Belief	Dominant North American culture is best.	Love your neighbor as yourself.

A congregational project would be a natural way to continue a theological conversation about money, long after completing this program. In discerning a project, leaders need to strike the right balance for their unique context. Leaders have the opportunity to infuse this material with a sense of urgency, immediacy, and practicality. He or she might find it helpful to survey the congregation again about Bible stories about money to discern the embedded theology of money and an appropriate project. Of course, there will not be a single perfect project, but the complex and messy work of discernment will likely produce congregational engagement, community standards, new money rules, and a glimpse of the Beloved Community.

Easter Week 6, Year C: Option 2 Forum and Exercise

The second forum for Easter week 6 will identify a congregational project that addresses global inequality. While the first option focuses on global issues that might be supported locally, the second option will evaluate ways of providing global support. The group should study the issues and systems that perpetuate inequality globally and offer opportunities for the congregation to discern how it might respond. Perhaps the congregation can ask what it means to love our neighbor as ourselves, when our neighbor is thousands of miles away. For example, the congregation could become involved with Amnesty International or another organization that protects human rights. It might join an international effort for economic justice.

	The Present	The Possibility
Behavior		Amnesty International
Belief		Love your neighbor as yourself.

As discussed above, the congregation must discuss and acknowledge its current behavior and beliefs if it hopes to genuinely move forward. This work—the project, and the self-evaluation and discernment that accompanies it—is not a single, perfect project but a demonstration of faith in action.

	The Present	The Possibility
Behavior	Protect the status quo.	Amnesty International
Belief	Dominant North American culture is best.	Love your neighbor as yourself.

CHAPTER

9

Conclusion

The last thing that clergy need is more work. There is plenty to do in churches already. Nevertheless, a key role for congregational leaders is to read and write about challenging topics, like money. While plenty of people write about money, few provoke a theological understanding of it. More importantly, as ordained members of the Church, when we work outside of our comfort zones, we have the opportunity to lead intentional conversations that can build community, hope, and love.

At Christ Church Cathedral in Nashville, in 2013, then-presiding bishop of the Episcopal Church, Katharine Jefferts Schori, delivered a sermon in which she acknowledged the tremendous difficulty that we have talking about money in the church, noting that many people see the topic of money as "the third rail."[1] Yet, an honest conversation about money is essential for healthy congregants, congregations, and denominations. Furthermore, it is essential if the church is ever going to be able to really lead on issues of economic justice and equity. Therefore,

1. "Presiding Bishop's Sermon at Christ Church Cathedral, Nashville," Episcopal digitalnetwork.com, accessed December 3, 2016, *http://episcopaldigitalnetwork.com/ens/2013/09/22/presiding-bishops-sermon-at-christ-church-cathedral-nashville*.

congregational leaders need to know how to lead theological discussions of money skillfully. While people are generally reluctant to engage in these conversations in church, many are intrigued when it is presented in new and practical ways.

Fortunately, Jews and Christians have been discussing money and providing guidance on its proper use for millennia, both in scripture and in theology. This book has attempted to provide a theological and scriptural basis for a discussion of money, and it has also attempted to provide some sample curricula for congregational leaders to lead those conversations, representing one approach to this topic. Any fruitful discourse about money must reflect the congregational leaders' own setting and leadership style. In addition, leaders must be prepared to face some resistance. Many people come to church on Sunday to be comforted, particularly during these challenging times, and a discussion about how Christians should consider and use their money might not be comforting. However, as Dr. Levinson has witnessed in her practice, most people are incredibly comforted once they start to face and name the complex set of emotions they have about money.[2] Leaders will need to regularly remind their congregations of the spiritual and theological importance of this work. Ultimately, our relationship with money does not need to hinder us. Grounding our view of money in a theological perspective can help transform us, moving us past our financial anxieties, connecting us more fully in the body of Christ, and enabling us to more fully become the people of God. Finally, these conversations require courage; leaders cannot pass it off to someone else. Congregational leaders need to be willing to talk dollars—and sense.

2. Levinson, *Emotional Currency*, 2–10.

Appendix

On a scale of 1 to 5, how often do you worry about paying your monthly bills? A score of 1 means that you worry a lot, and 5 means that you do not worry at all.

St. Stephen's parishioners, 2019

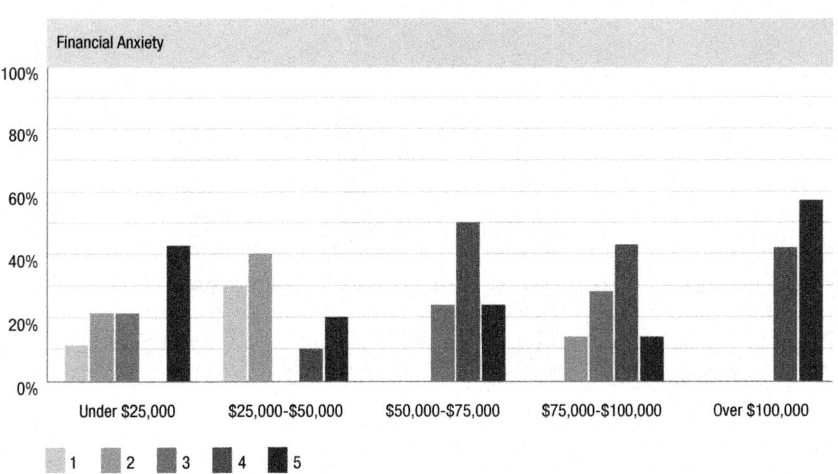

N=41; Source: St. Stephen's Theology & Money Survey, January 2019

Financial Anxiety							
	1	2	3	4	5	TOTAL	WEIGHTED AVERAGE
Under $25,000	11.11% 1	22.22% 2	22.22% 2	0.00% 0	44.44% 4	21.95% 9	3.44
$25,000-$50,000	30.00% 3	40.00% 4	0.00% 0	10.00% 1	20.00% 2	24.39% 10	2.50
$50,000-$75,000	0.00% 0	0.00% 0	25.00% 2	50.00% 4	25.00% 2	19.51% 8	4.00
$75,000-$100,000	0.00% 0	14.29% 1	28.57% 2	42.86% 3	41.29% 1	17.07% 7	3.57
Over $100,000	0.00% 0	0.00% 0	0.00% 0	42.86% 3	57.14% 4	17.07% 7	4.57

N=41; Source: St. Stephen's Theology & Money Survey, January 2019

On a scale of 1 to 5, how often do you worry about paying your monthly bills? A score of 1 means that you worry a lot, and 5 means that you do not worry at all.

St. Francis's parishioners, 2020

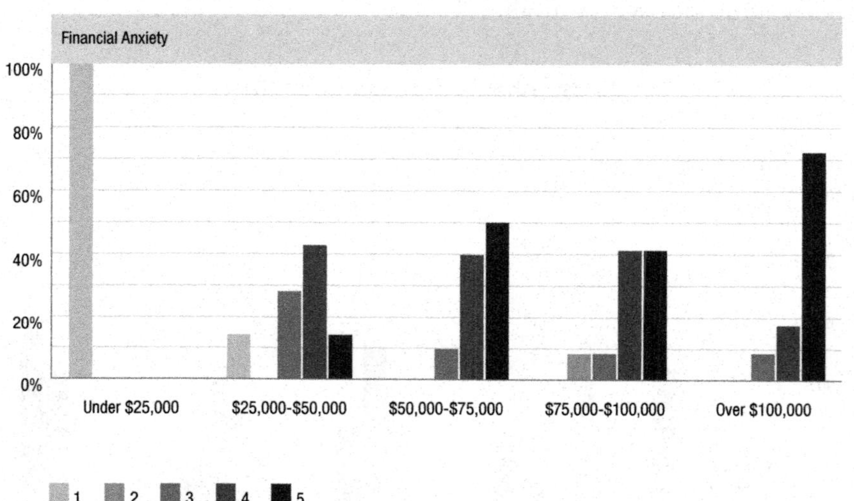

N=41; Source: St. Francis Theology & Money Survey, July 2020

Financial Anxiety

	1	2	3	4	5	TOTAL	WEIGHTED AVERAGE
Under $25,000	100.00% 1	0.00% 0	0.00% 0	0.00% 0	0.00% 0	2.44% 1	1.00
$25,000-$50,000	14.29% 1	0.00% 0	28.57% 2	42.86% 3	14.29% 1	17.07% 7	3.43
$50,000-$75,000	0.00% 0	0.00% 0	10.00% 1	40.00% 4	50.00% 5	24.39% 10	4.40
$75,000-$100,000	0.00% 0	8.33% 1	8.33% 1	41.67% 5	41.67% 5	29.27% 12	4.17
Over $100,000	0.00% 0	0.00% 0	9.09% 1	18.18% 2	27.73% 8	26.83% 11	4.64

N=41; Source: St. Francis Theology & Money Survey, July 2020

On a scale of 1 to 5, how often do you worry about paying your monthly bills? A score of 1 means that you worry a lot, and 5 means that you do not worry at all.

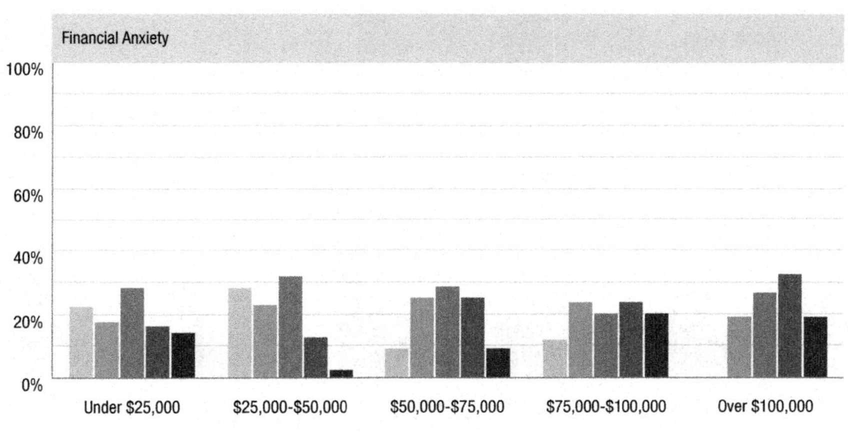

N=202; Source: Self-identified Christians in Survey Monkey Survey, April 2019

Financial Anxiety	1	2	3	4	5	TOTAL	WEIGHTED AVERAGE
Under $25,000	23.21% 13	17.86% 10	28.57% 16	16.07% 9	14.29% 8	27.72% 56	2.80
$25,000-$50,000	28.57% 14	24.49% 12	32.65% 16	12.24% 6	2.04% 1	24.26% 49	2.35
$50,000-$75,000	9.68% 3	25.81% 8	29.03% 9	25.81% 8	9.68% 3	15.35% 31	3.00
$75,000-$100,000	12.00% 3	24.00% 6	20.00% 5	24.00% 6	20.00% 5	12.38% 25	3.16
Over $100,000	0.00% 0	19.51% 8	26.83% 11	34.15% 14	19.51% 8	20.30% 41	3.54

N=202; Source: Self-identified Christians in Survey Monkey Survey, April 2019

On a scale of 1 to 5, how often do you worry about paying your monthly bills? A score of 1 means that you worry a lot, and 5 means that you do not worry at all.

Self-identified Christians, 2020

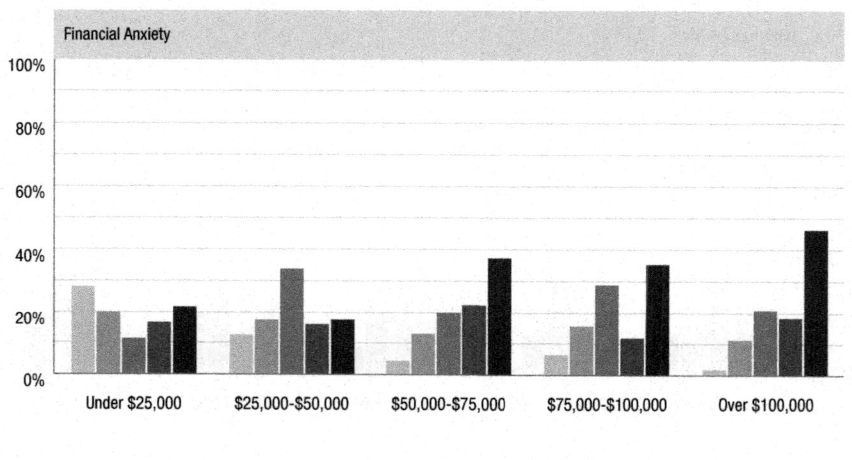

N=211; Source: Self-identified Christians in Survey Monkey Survey, July 2020

Financial Anxiety	1	2	3	4	5	TOTAL	WEIGHTED AVERAGE
Under $25,000	28.57% 10	20.00% 7	11.43% 4	17.14% 6	22.86% 8	16.59% 35	2.86
$25,000-$50,000	13.43% 9	17.91% 12	34.33% 23	16.42% 11	17.91% 12	31.75% 67	3.07
$50,000-$75,000	5.71% 2	14.29% 5	20.00% 7	22.86% 8	37.14% 13	16.59% 35	3.71
$75,000-$100,000	6.45% 2	16.13% 5	20.03% 9	12.90% 4	35.48% 11	14.69% 31	3.55
Over $100,000	2.33% 1	11.63% 5	20.93% 9	18.60% 8	46.51% 20	20.38% 43	3.95

N=211; Source: Self-identified Christians in Survey Monkey Survey, July 2020

On a scale of 1 to 5, how much worry or fear do you experience about money? A score of 1 means a lot of worry or fear, and 5 means no worry or fear.

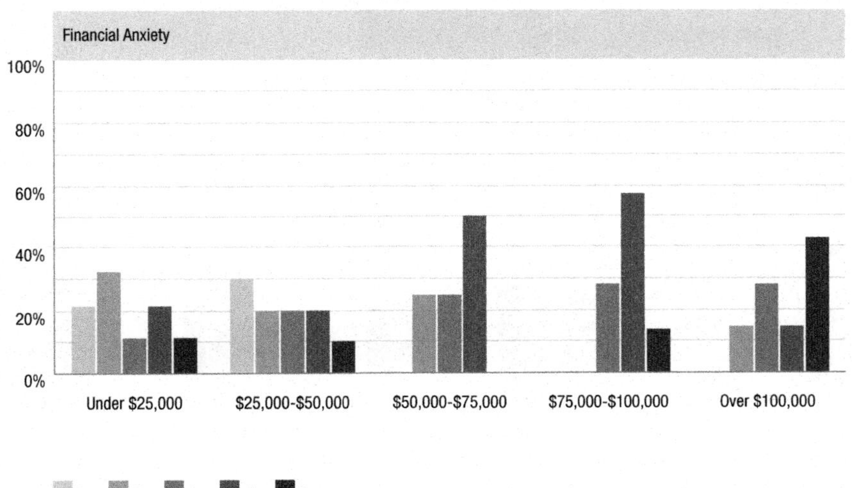

N=41; Source: St. Stephen's Theology & Money Survey, January 2019

Financial Anxiety

	1	2	3	4	5	TOTAL	WEIGHTED AVERAGE
Under $25,000	22.22% 2	33.33% 3	11.11% 1	22.22% 2	11.11% 1	21.95% 9	2.67
$25,000-$50,000	30.00% 3	20.00% 2	20.00% 2	20.00% 2	10.00% 1	24.39% 10	2.60
$50,000-$75,000	0.00% 0	25.00% 2	25.00% 2	50.00% 4	0.00% 0	19.51% 8	3.25
$75,000-$100,000	0.00% 0	0.00% 0	20.57% 2	57.14% 4	14.29% 1	17.07% 7	3.86
Over $100,000	0.00% 0	14.29% 1	28.57% 2	14.29% 1	42.86% 3	17.07% 7	3.86

N=41; Source: St. Stephen's Theology & Money Survey, January 2019

On a scale of 1 to 5, how much worry or fear do you experience about money? A score of 1 means a lot of worry or fear, and 5 means no worry or fear.

St. Francis's parishioners, 2020

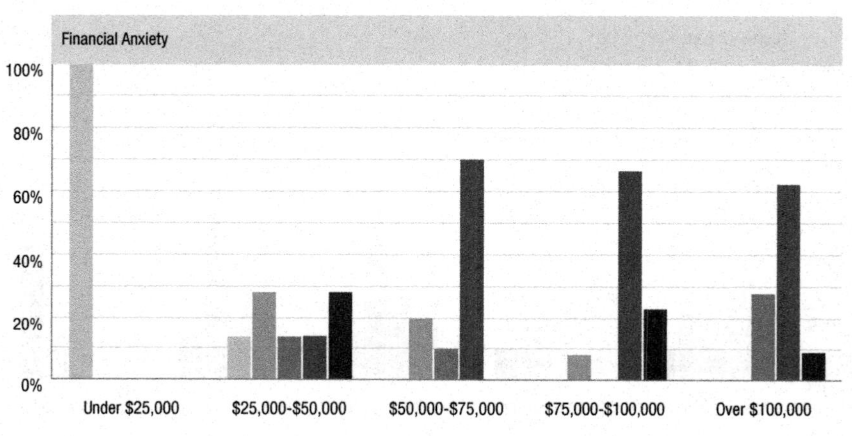

N=41; Source: St. Francis Theology & Money Survey, July 2020

Financial Anxiety

	1	2	3	4	5	TOTAL	WEIGHTED AVERAGE
Under $25,000	100.00% 1	0.00% 0	0.00% 0	0.00% 0	0.00% 0	2.44% 1	1.00
$25,000-$50,000	14.29% 1	28.57% 2	14.29% 1	14.29% 1	28.57% 2	17.07% 7	3.14
$50,000-$75,000	0.00% 0	20.00% 2	10.00% 1	70.00% 7	0.00% 0	24.39% 10	3.50
$75,000-$100,000	0.00% 0	8.33% 1	0.00% 0	66.67% 8	25.00% 3	29.27% 12	4.08
Over $100,000	0.00% 0	0.00% 0	27.27% 3	63.64% 7	9.09% 1	26.83% 11	3.82

N=41; Source: St. Francis Theology & Money Survey, July 2020

On a scale of 1 to 5, how much worry or fear do you experience about money? A score of 1 means a lot of worry or fear, and 5 means no worry or fear.

Self-identified Christians, 2019

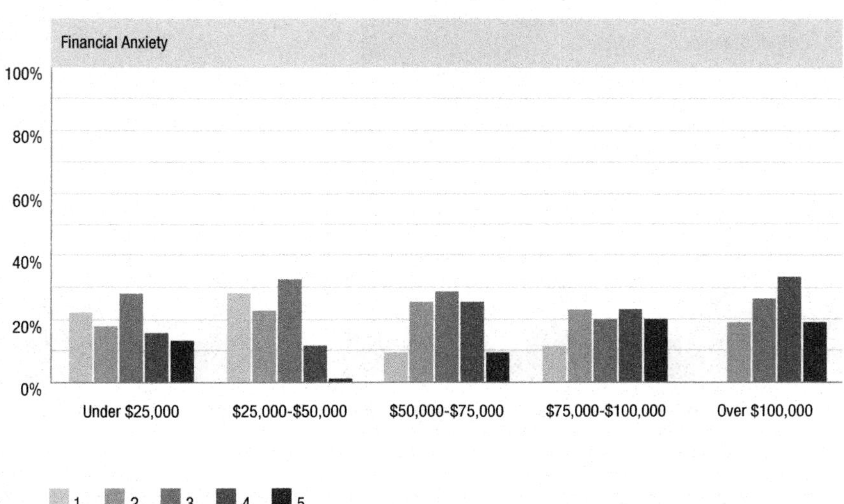

N=202; Source: Self-identified Christians in Survey Monkey Survey, April 2019

Financial Anxiety

	1	2	3	4	5	TOTAL	WEIGHTED AVERAGE
Under $25,000	23.21% 13	17.86% 10	28.57% 16	16.07% 9	14.29% 8	27.72% 56	2.80
$25,000-$50,000	28.57% 14	24.49% 12	32.65% 16	12.24% 6	2.04% 1	24.26% 49	2.35
$50,000-$75,000	9.68% 3	25.81% 8	29.03% 9	25.81% 8	9.68% 3	15.35% 31	3.00
$75,000-$100,000	12.00% 3	24.00% 6	20.00% 5	24.00% 6	20.00% 5	12.38% 25	3.16
Over $100,000	0.00% 0	19.51% 8	26.83% 11	34.15% 14	19.51% 8	20.30% 41	3.54

N=202; Source: Self-identified Christians in Survey Monkey Survey, April 2019

On a scale of 1 to 5, how much worry or fear do you experience about money? A score of 1 means a lot of worry or fear, and 5 means no worry or fear.

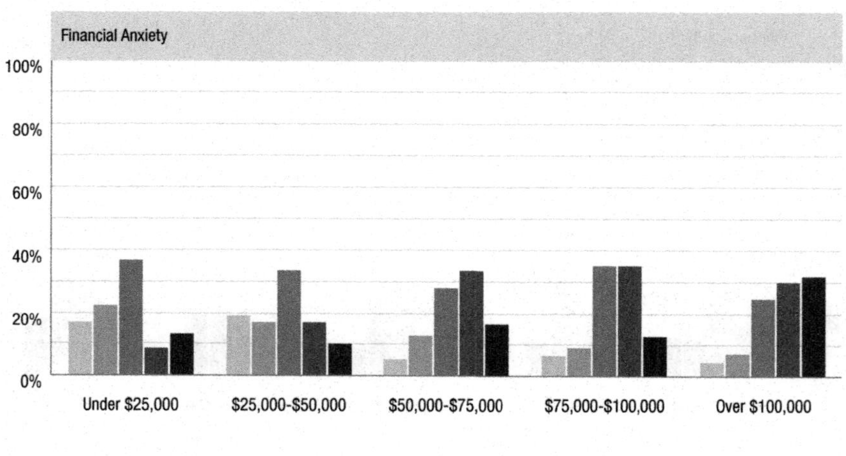

N=211; Source: Self-identified Christians in Survey Monkey Survey, July 2020

Financial Anxiety	1	2	3	4	5	TOTAL	WEIGHTED AVERAGE
Under $25,000	17.14% 6	22.86% 8	37.14% 13	8.57% 3	14.29% 5	16.59% 35	2.80
$25,000-$50,000	19.40% 13	17.91% 12	34.33% 23	17.91% 12	10.45% 7	31.75% 67	2.82
$50,000-$75,000	5.71% 2	14.29% 5	28.57% 10	34.29% 12	17.14% 6	16.59% 35	3.43
$75,000-$100,000	6.45% 2	9.68% 3	35.48% 11	35.48% 11	12.90% 4	14.69% 31	3.39
Over $100,000	4.65% 2	6.98% 3	25.58% 11	30.23% 13	32.56% 14	20.38% 43	3.79

N=211; Source: Self-identified Christians in Survey Monkey Survey, July 2020

On a scale of 1 to 5, how important is theology in your daily decisions about how you spend your money? A score of 1 means very little consideration and 5 means a lot of consideration of theology in your daily decisions about how you spend your money.

St. Stephen's parishioners, 2019

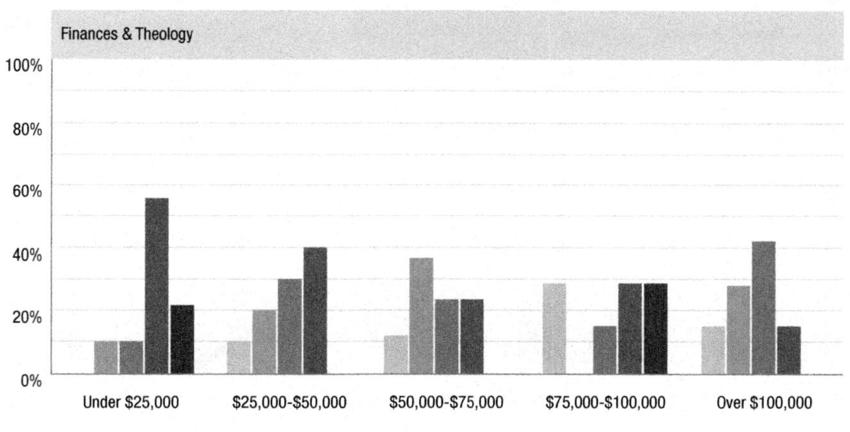

N=41; Source: St. Stephen's Theology & Money Survey, January 2019

Finances & Theology

	1	2	3	4	5	TOTAL	WEIGHTED AVERAGE
Under $25,000	0.00% 0	11.11% 1	11.11% 1	55.56% 5	22.22% 2	21.95% 9	3.89
$25,000-$50,000	10.00% 1	20.00% 2	30.00% 3	40.00% 4	0.00% 0	24.39% 10	3.00
$50,000-$75,000	12.50% 1	37.50% 3	25.00% 2	25.00% 2	0.00% 0	19.51% 8	2.63
$75,000-$100,000	28.57% 2	0.00% 0	14.29% 1	28.57% 2	28.57% 2	17.07% 7	3.29
Over $100,000	4.29% 1	28.57% 2	42.86% 3	14.29% 1	0.00% 0	17.07% 7	2.57

N=41; Source: St. Stephen's Theology & Money Survey, January 2019

On a scale of 1 to 5, how important is theology in your daily decisions about how you spend your money? A score of 1 means very little consideration and 5 means a lot of consideration of theology in your daily decisions about how you spend your money.

St. Francis's parishioners, July 2020

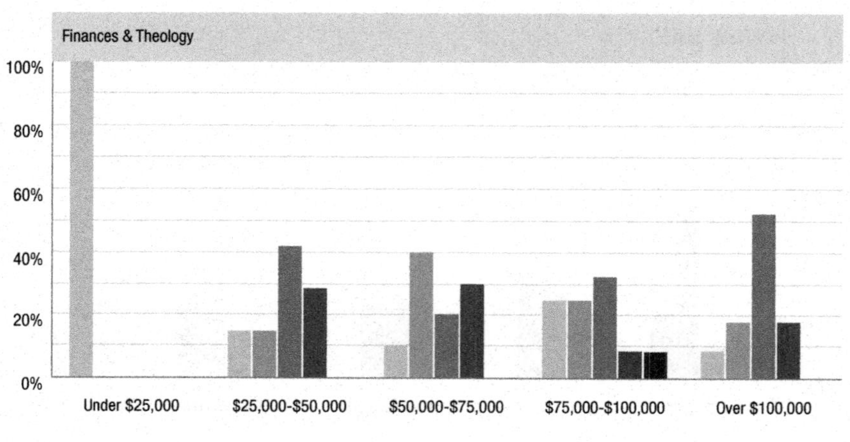

1 2 3 4 5

N=41; Source: St. Francis Theology & Money Survey, July 2020

Finances & Theology							
	1	2	3	4	5	TOTAL	WEIGHTED AVERAGE
Under $25,000	100.00% 1	0.00% 0	0.00% 0	0.00% 0	0.00% 0	2.44% 1	1.00
$25,000-$50,000	14.29% 1	14.29% 1	42.86% 3	28.57% 2	0.00% 0	17.07% 7	2.86
$50,000-$75,000	10.00% 1	40.00% 4	20.00% 2	30.00% 3	0.00% 0	24.39% 10	2.70
$75,000-$100,000	25.00% 3	25.00% 3	33.33% 4	8.33% 1	8.33% 1	29.27% 12	2.50
Over $100,000	9.09% 1	18.18% 2	54.55% 6	18.18% 2	0.00% 0	26.83% 11	2.82

N=41; Source: St. Francis Theology & Money Survey, July 2020

On a scale of 1 to 5, how important is theology in your daily decisions about how you spend your money? A score of 1 means very little consideration and 5 means a lot of consideration of theology in your daily decisions about how you spend your money.

Self-identified Christians, 2019

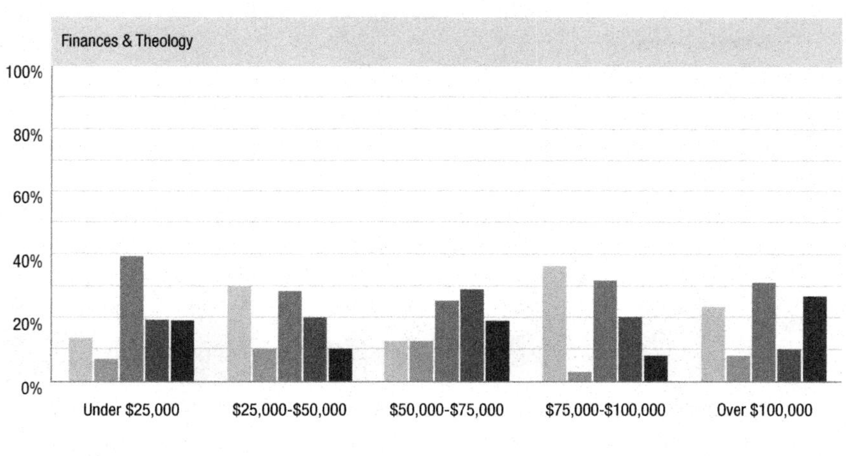

N=202; Source: Self-identified Christians in Survey Monkey Survey, April 2019

Finances & Theology

	1	2	3	4	5	TOTAL	WEIGHTED AVERAGE
Under $25,000	14.29% 8	7.14% 4	39.29% 22	19.64% 11	19.64% 11	27.72% 56	3.23
$25,000-$50,000	30.61% 15	10.20% 5	28.57% 14	20.41% 10	10.20% 5	24.26% 49	2.69
$50,000-$75,000	12.90% 4	12.90% 4	25.81% 8	29.03% 9	19.35% 6	15.35% 31	3.29
$75,000-$100,000	36.00% 9	4.00% 1	32.00% 8	20.00% 5	8.00% 2	12.38% 25	2.60
Over $100,000	24.39% 10	7.32% 3	31.71% 13	9.76% 4	26.83% 11	20.30% 41	3.07

N=202; Source: Self-identified Christians in Survey Monkey Survey, April 2019

On a scale of 1 to 5, how important is theology in your daily decisions about how you spend your money? A score of 1 means very little consideration and 5 means a lot of consideration of theology in your daily decisions about how you spend your money.

Self-identified Christians, 2020

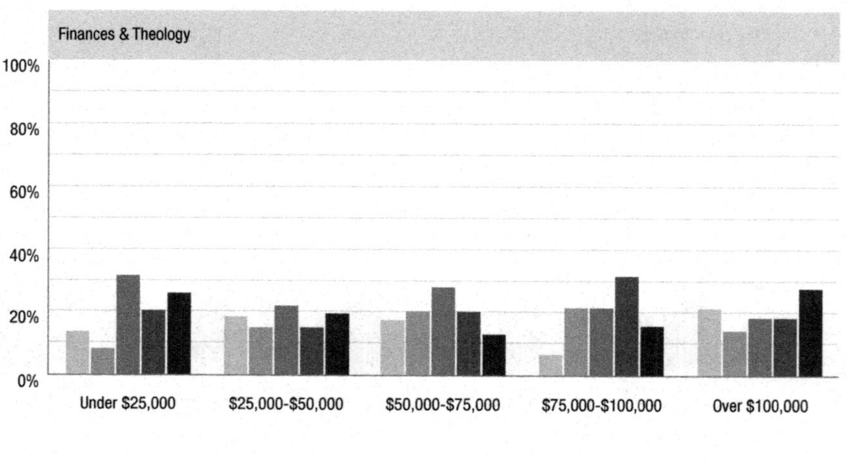

N=211; Source: Self-identified Christians in Survey Monkey Survey, July 2020

Finances & Theology	1	2	3	4	5	TOTAL	WEIGHTED AVERAGE
Under $25,000	14.29% 5	8.75% 3	31.43% 11	20.00% 7	25.71% 9	16.59% 35	3.34
$25,000-$50,000	17.91% 12	14.93% 10	32.84% 22	14.93% 10	19.40% 13	31.75% 67	3.03
$50,000-$75,000	17.14% 6	20.00% 7	28.57% 10	20.00% 7	14.29% 5	16.59% 35	2.94
$75,000-$100,000	6.45% 2	22.58% 7	22.58% 7	32.26% 10	16.13% 5	14.69% 31	3.29
Over $100,000	20.93% 9	13.95% 6	18.60% 8	18.60% 8	27.91% 12	20.38% 43	3.19

N=211; Source: Self-identified Christians in Survey Monkey, July 2020

How open are you to hearing about theology and the daily use of money during worship services at your religious institution? A score of 1 means no interest and 5 means a lot of interest in hearing about the daily use of money at worship services.

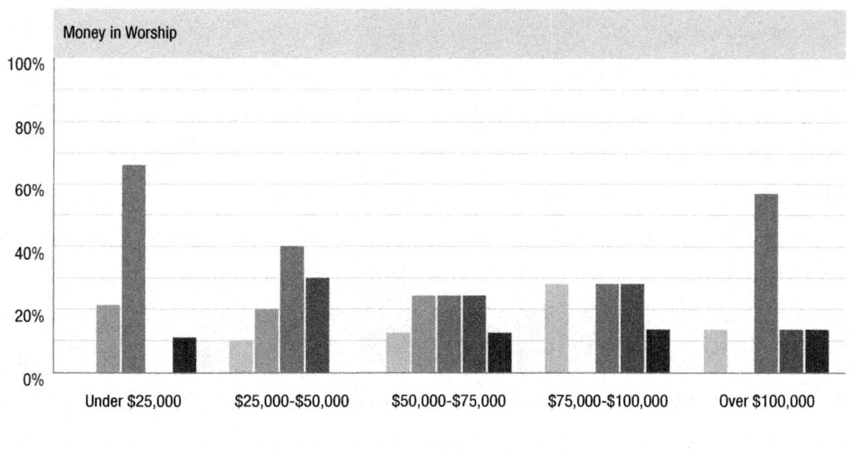

Money in Worship

	1	2	3	4	5	TOTAL	WEIGHTED AVERAGE
Under $25,000	0.00% 0	22.22% 2	66.67% 6	0.00% 0	11.11% 1	21.95% 9	3.00
$25,000-$50,000	10.00% 1	20.00% 2	40.00% 4	30.00% 3	0.00% 0	24.39% 10	2.90
$50,000-$75,000	12.50% 1	25.00% 2	25.00% 2	25.00% 2	12.50% 1	19.51% 8	3.00
$75,000-$100,000	28.57% 2	0.00% 0	28.57% 2	28.57% 2	14.29% 1	17.07% 7	3.00
Over $100,000	14.29% 1	0.00% 0	57.14% 4	14.29% 1	14.29% 1	17.07% 7	3.14

N=41; Source: St. Stephen's Theology & Money Survey, January 2019

How open are you to hearing about theology and the daily use of money during worship services at your religious institution? A score of 1 means no interest and 5 means a lot of interest in hearing about the daily use of money at worship services.

St. Francis's parishioners, 2019

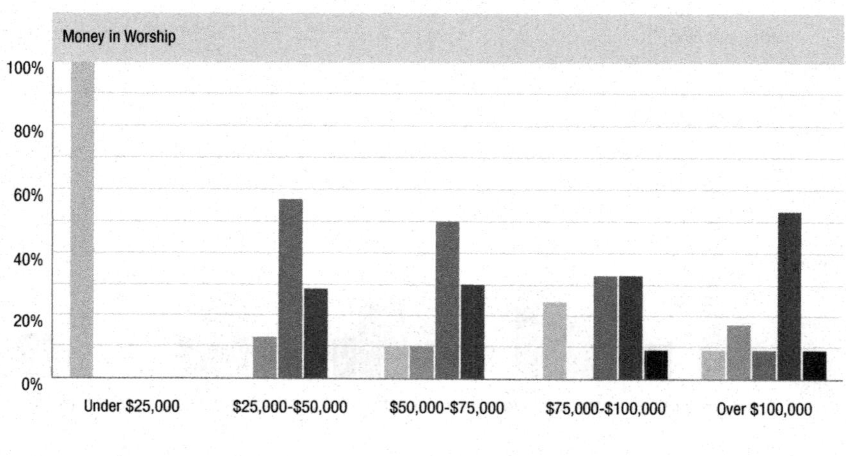

N=41; Source: St. Francis Theology & Money Survey, January 2019

Money in Worship

	1	2	3	4	5	TOTAL	WEIGHTED AVERAGE
Under $25,000	100.00% 1	0.00% 0	0.00% 0	0.00% 0	0.00% 0	2.44% 1	1.00
$25,000-$50,000	0.00% 0	14.29% 1	57.14% 4	28.57% 2	0.00% 0	17.07% 7	3.14
$50,000-$75,000	10.00% 1	10.00% 1	50.00% 5	30.00% 3	0.00% 0	24.39% 10	3.00
$75,000-$100,000	25.00% 3	0.00% 0	33.33% 4	33.33% 4	8.33% 1	29.27% 12	3.00
Over $100,000	9.09% 1	18.18% 2	9.09% 1	54.55% 6	9.09% 1	26.83% 11	3.36

N=41; Source: St. Francis Theology & Money Survey, January 2019

How open are you to hearing about theology and the daily use of money during worship services at your religious institution? A score of 1 means no interest and 5 means a lot of interest in hearing about the daily use of money at worship services.

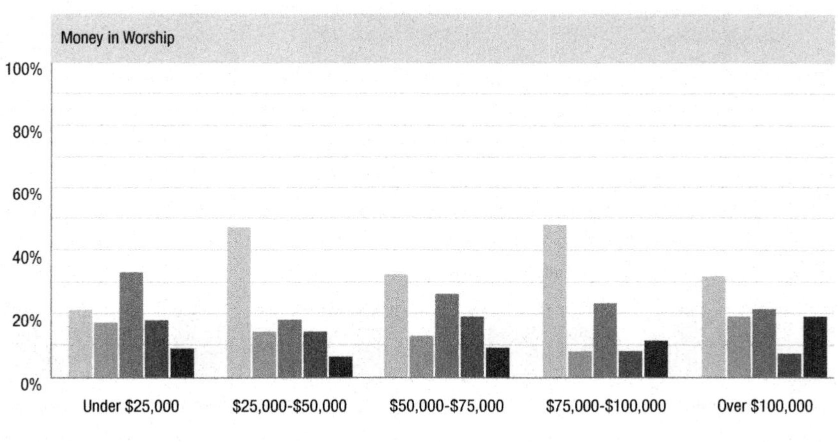

N=202; Source: Self-identified Christians in Survey Monkey Survey, April 2019

Money in Worship

	1	2	3	4	5	TOTAL	WEIGHTED AVERAGE
Under $25,000	21.43% 12	17.86% 10	33.93% 19	17.86% 10	8.93% 5	27.72% 56	2.75
$25,000-$50,000	46.94% 23	14.29% 7	18.37% 9	14.29% 7	6.12% 3	24.26% 49	2.18
$50,000-$75,000	32.26% 10	12.90% 4	25.81% 8	19.35% 6	9.68% 3	15.35% 31	2.61
$75,000-$100,000	48.00% 12	8.00% 2	24.00% 6	8.00% 2	12.00% 3	12.38% 25	2.28
Over $100,000	31.71% 13	19.51% 8	21.95% 9	7.32% 3	19.51% 8	20.30% 41	2.63

N=202; Source: Self-identified Christians in Survey Monkey Survey, April 2019

How open are you to hearing about theology and the daily use of money during worship services at your religious institution? A score of 1 means no interest and 5 means a lot of interest in hearing about the daily use of money at worship services.

Self-identified Christians, 2020

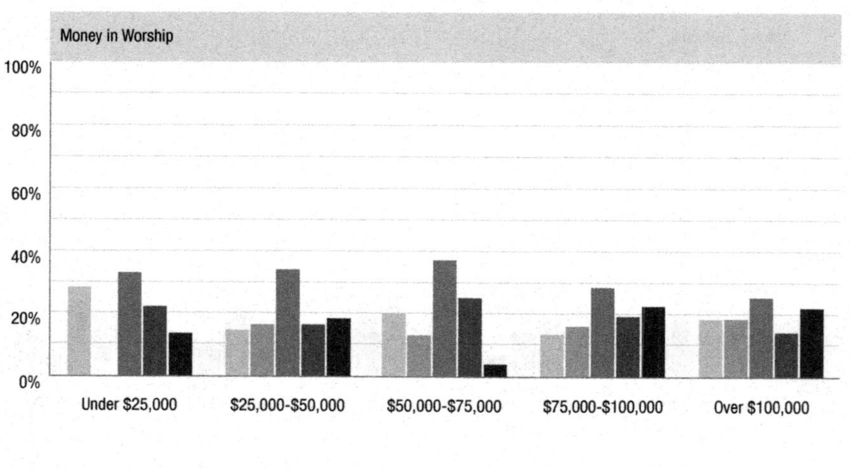

1 2 3 4 5

N=211; Source: Self-identified Christians in Survey Monkey, July 2020

Money in Worship

	1	2	3	4	5	TOTAL	WEIGHTED AVERAGE
Under $25,000	28.57% 10	0.00% 0	34.29% 12	22.86% 8	14.29% 5	16.59% 35	2.94
$25,000-$50,000	14.93% 10	16.42% 11	34.33% 23	16.42% 11	17.91% 12	31.75% 67	3.06
$50,000-$75,000	20.00% 7	11.43% 4	37.14% 13	25.71% 9	5.71% 2	16.59% 35	2.86
$75,000-$100,000	12.90% 4	16.13% 5	29.03% 9	19.35% 6	22.58% 7	14.69% 31	3.23
Over $100,000	18.60% 8	18.60% 8	25.58% 11	13.95% 6	23.26% 10	20.38% 43	3.05

N=211; Source: Self-identified Christians in Survey Monkey, July 2020

How open are you to hearing about theology and the daily use of money during worship services at your religious institution? A score of 1 means no interest and 5 means a lot of interest in hearing about the daily use of money at worship services.

Clergy, 2020

Theology of Money in Worship

Answered: 29 Skipped: 2

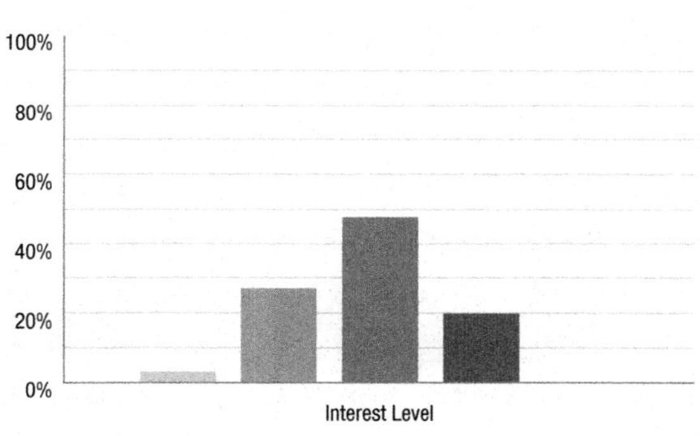

	1	2	3	4	5	TOTAL	WEIGHTED AVERAGE
Interest Level	3.45% 1	27.59% 8	48.28% 14	20.69% 6	0.00% 0	29	2.86

N=29; Source: Oregon Diocese Clergy Survey, July 2020

How likely would you be to attend a class at a religious institution that focused on theology and your daily use of money? A score of 1 means unlikely to attend and 5 means very likely to attend a class on theology and your daily use of money.

St. Stephen's parishioners, 2019

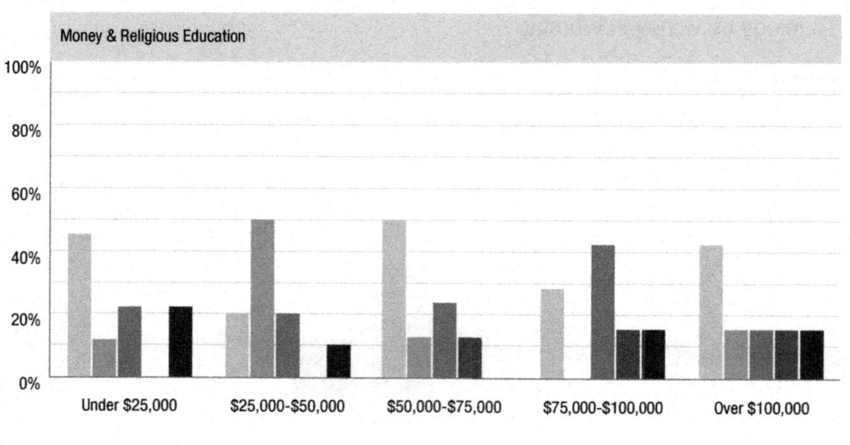

1 2 3 4 5

N=41; Source: St. Stephen's Theology & Money Survey, January 2019

Money & Religious Education

	1	2	3	4	5	TOTAL	WEIGHTED AVERAGE
Under $25,000	44.44% 4	11.11% 1	22.22% 2	0.00% 0	22.22% 2	21.95% 9	2.44
$25,000-$50,000	20.00% 2	50.00% 5	20.00% 2	0.00% 0	10.00% 1	24.39% 10	2.30
$50,000-$75,000	50.00% 4	12.50% 1	25.00% 2	12.50% 1	0.00% 0	19.51% 8	2.00
$75,000-$100,000	28.57% 2	0.00% 0	42.86% 3	14.29% 1	14.29% 1	17.07% 7	2.86
Over $100,000	42.86% 3	14.29% 1	14.29% 1	14.29% 1	14.26% 1	17.07% 7	2.43

N=41; Source: St. Stephen's Theology & Money Survey, January 2019

How likely would you be to attend a class at a religious institution that focused on theology and your daily use of money? A score of 1 means unlikely to attend and 5 means very likely to attend a class on theology and your daily use of money.

St. Francis's parishioners, 2019

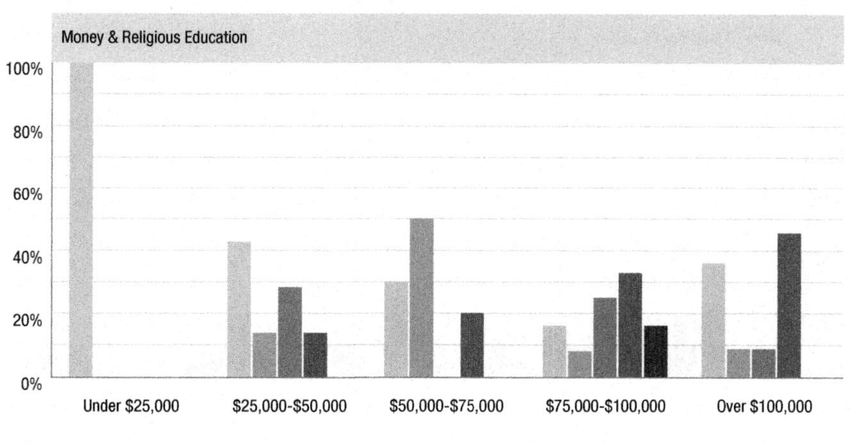

N=41; Source: St. Francis Theology & Money Survey, July 2020

Money & Religious Education							
	1	2	3	4	5	TOTAL	WEIGHTED AVERAGE
Under $25,000	100.00% 1	0.00% 0	0.00% 0	0.00% 0	0.00% 0	2.44% 1	1.00
$25,000-$50,000	42.86% 3	14.29% 1	28.57% 2	14.29% 1	0.00% 0	17.07% 7	2.14
$50,000-$75,000	30.00% 3	50.00% 5	0.00% 0	20.00% 2	0.00% 0	24.39% 10	2.10
$75,000-$100,000	16.67% 2	8.33% 1	25.00% 3	33.33% 4	16.67% 2	29.27% 12	3.25
Over $100,000	36.36% 4	9.09% 1	9.09% 1	45.45% 5	0.00% 0	26.83% 11	2.64

N=41; Source: St. Francis Theology & Money Survey, July 2020

How likely would you be to attend a class at a religious institution that focused on theology and your daily use of money? A score of 1 means unlikely to attend and 5 means very likely to attend a class on theology and your daily use of money.

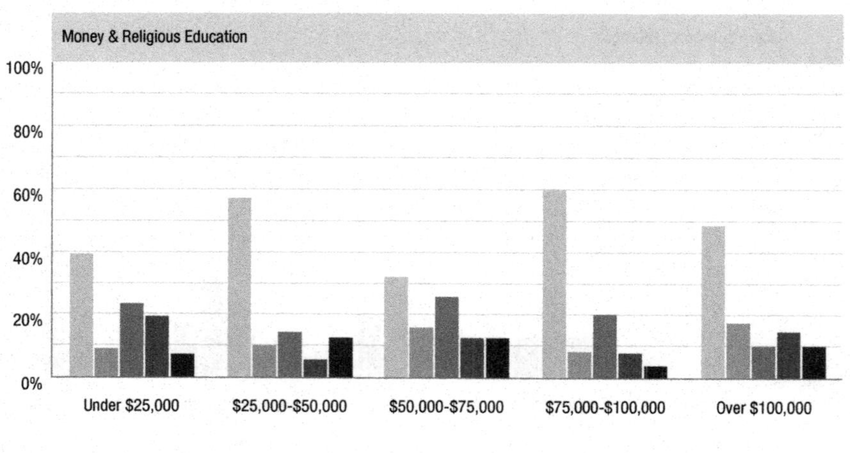

N=202; Source: Self-identified Christians in Survey Monkey Survey, April 2019

Money & Religious Education

	1	2	3	4	5	TOTAL	WEIGHTED AVERAGE
Under $25,000	39.29% 22	8.93% 5	25.00% 14	19.64% 11	7.14% 4	27.72% 56	2.46
$25,000-$50,000	57.14% 28	10.20% 5	14.29% 7	6.12% 3	12.24% 6	24.26% 49	2.06
$50,000-$75,000	32.26% 10	16.13% 5	25.81% 8	12.90% 4	12.90% 4	15.35% 31	2.58
$75,000-$100,000	60.00% 15	8.00% 2	20.00% 5	8.00% 2	4.00% 1	12.38% 25	1.88
Over $100,000	48.78% 20	17.07% 7	9.76% 4	14.63% 6	9.76% 4	20.30% 41	2.20

N=202; Source: Self-identified Christians in Survey Monkey Survey, April 2019

How likely would you be to attend a class at a religious institution that focused on theology and your daily use of money? A score of 1 means unlikely to attend and 5 means very likely to attend a class on theology and your daily use of money.

Self-identified Christians, 2019

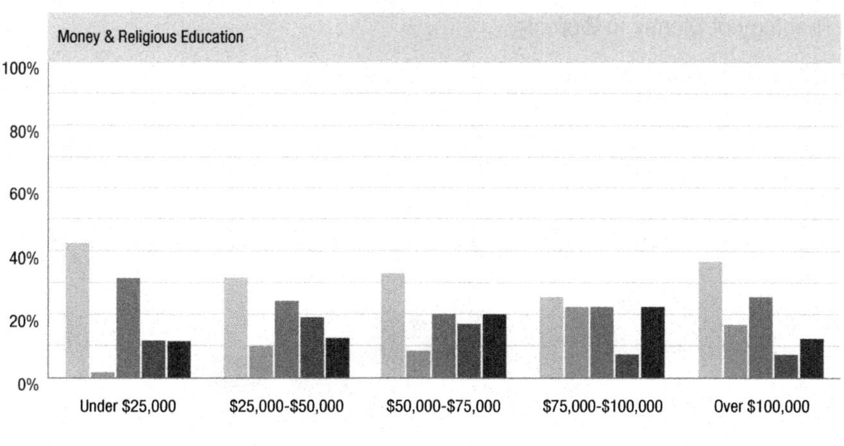

N=211; Source: Self-identified Christians in Survey Monkey Survey, July 2020

Money & Religious Education							
	1	2	3	4	5	TOTAL	WEIGHTED AVERAGE
Under $25,000	42.86% 15	2.86% 1	31.43% 11	11.43% 4	11.43% 4	16.59% 35	2.46
$25,000-$50,000	31.34% 21	10.45% 7	25.37% 17	19.40% 13	13.43% 9	31.75% 67	2.73
$50,000-$75,000	34.29% 12	8.57% 3	20.00% 7	17.14% 6	20.00% 7	16.59% 35	2.80
$75,000-$100,000	25.81% 8	22.58% 7	22.58% 7	6.45% 2	22.58% 7	14.69% 31	2.77
Over $100,000	37.21% 16	16.28% 7	25.58% 11	6.98% 3	13.95% 6	20.38% 43	2.44

N=211; Source: Self-identified Christians in Survey Monkey Survey, July 2020

How likely would you be to attend a class at a religious institution that focused on theology and your daily use of money? A score of 1 means unlikely to attend and 5 means very likely to attend a class on theology and your daily use of money.

Clergy, 2020

Theology of Money in Worship

Answered: 29 Skipped: 2

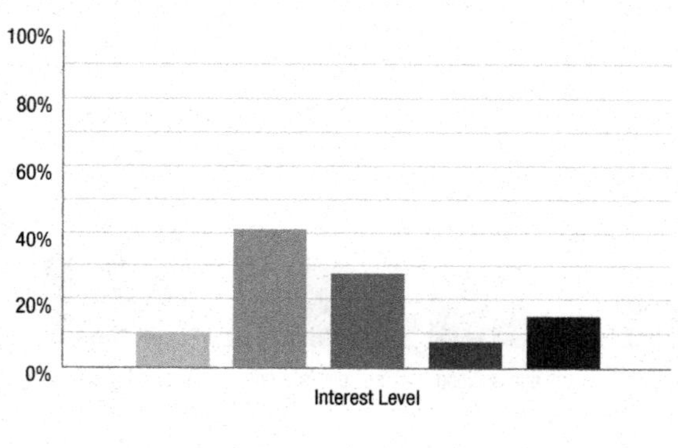

	1	2	3	4	5	TOTAL	WEIGHTED AVERAGE
Interest Level	10.34% 3	41.38% 12	27.59% 8	6.90% 2	13.79% 4	29	2.72

N=29; Source: Oregon Diocese Clergy Survey, July 2020

When making daily decisions about how you spend your money, how helpful would it be to think about spending your money in ways that are creative, redemptive, and sustaining? A score of 1 means not helpful and 5 means very helpful to think about spending your money in terms of things that are creative, redemptive, and sustaining.

St. Stephen's parishioners, 2019

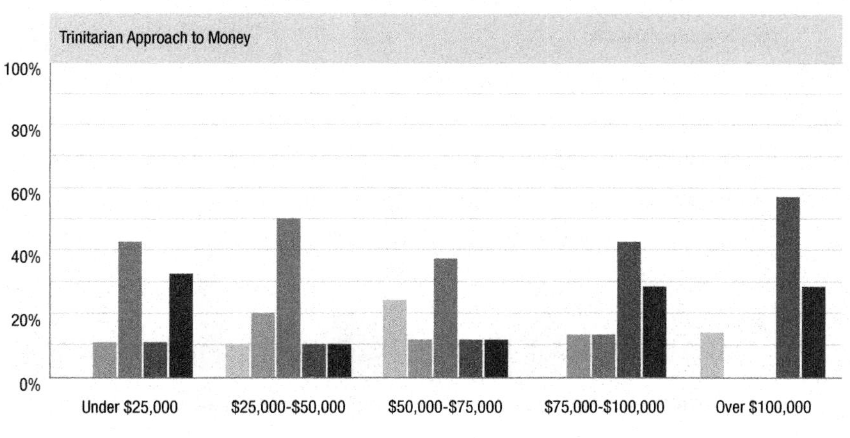

N=41; Source: St. Stephen's Theology & Money Survey, January 2019

Trinitarian Approach to Money	1	2	3	4	5	TOTAL	WEIGHTED AVERAGE
Under $25,000	0.00% 0	11.11% 1	44.44% 4	11.11% 1	33.33% 3	21.95% 9	3.67
$25,000-$50,000	10.00% 1	20.00% 2	50.00% 5	10.00% 1	10.00% 1	24.39% 10	2.90
$50,000-$75,000	25.00% 2	12.50% 1	37.50% 3	12.50% 1	12.50% 1	19.51% 8	2.75
$75,000-$100,000	0.00% 0	14.29% 1	14.29% 1	42.86% 3	28.57% 2	17.07% 7	3.86
Over $100,000	14.29% 1	0.00% 0	0.00% 0	57.14% 4	28.57% 2	17.07% 7	3.86

N=41; Source: St. Stephen's Theology & Money Survey, January 2019

When making daily decisions about how you spend your money, how helpful would it be to think about spending your money in ways that are creative, redemptive, and sustaining? A score of 1 means not helpful and 5 means very helpful to think about spending your money in terms of things that are creative, redemptive, and sustaining.

St. Francis's parishioners, 2020

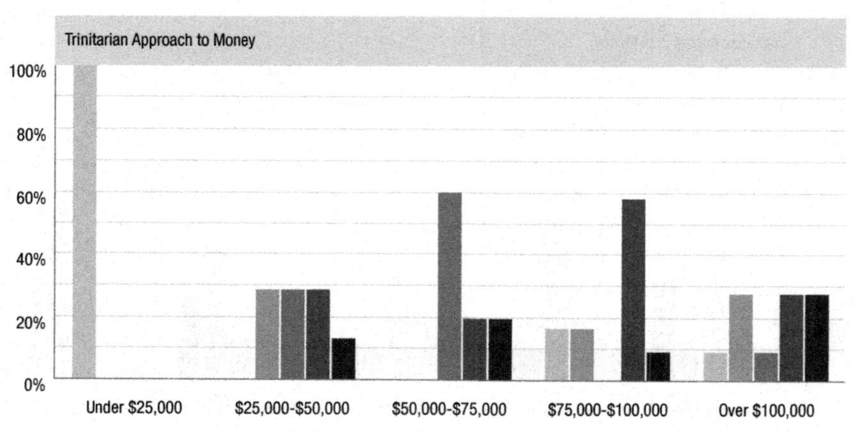

N=41; Source: St. Francis Theology & Money Survey, July 2020

Trinitarian Approach to Money

	1	2	3	4	5	TOTAL	WEIGHTED AVERAGE
Under $25,000	100.00% 1	0.00% 0	0.00% 0	0.00% 0	0.00% 0	2.44% 1	1.00
$25,000-$50,000	0.00% 0	28.57% 2	28.57% 2	28.57% 2	14.29% 1	17.07% 7	3.29
$50,000-$75,000	0.00% 0	0.00% 0	60.00% 6	20.00% 2	20.00% 2	24.39% 10	3.60
$75,000-$100,000	16.67% 2	16.67% 2	0.00% 0	58.33% 7	8.33% 1	29.27% 12	3.25
Over $100,000	9.09% 1	27.27% 3	9.09% 1	27.27% 3	27.27% 3	26.83% 11	3.36

N=41; Source: St. Francis Theology & Money Survey, July 2020

When making daily decisions about how you spend your money, how helpful would it be to think about spending your money in ways that are creative, redemptive, and sustaining? A score of 1 means not helpful and 5 means very helpful to think about spending your money in terms of things that are creative, redemptive, and sustaining.

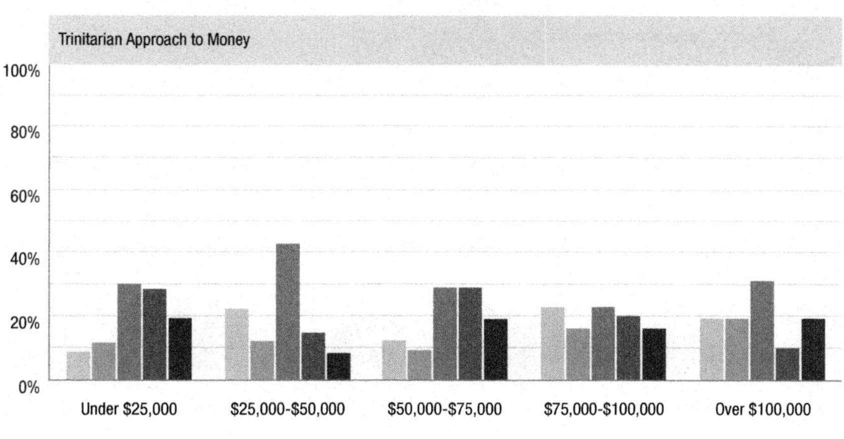

N=202; Source: Self-identified Christians in Survey Monkey Survey, April 2019

Trinitarian Approach to Money

	1	2	3	4	5	TOTAL	WEIGHTED AVERAGE
Under $25,000	8.93% 5	12.50% 7	30.36% 17	28.57% 16	19.64% 11	27.72% 56	3.38
$25,000-$50,000	22.45% 11	12.24% 6	42.86% 21	14.29% 7	8.16% 4	24.26% 49	2.73
$50,000-$75,000	12.90% 4	9.68% 3	29.03% 9	29.03% 9	19.35% 6	15.35% 31	3.32
$75,000-$100,000	24.00% 6	16.00% 4	24.00% 6	20.00% 5	16.00% 4	12.38% 25	2.88
Over $100,000	19.51% 8	19.51% 8	31.71% 13	9.76% 4	19.51% 8	20.30% 41	2.90

N=202; Source: Self-identified Christians in Survey Monkey Survey, April 2019

When making daily decisions about how you spend your money, how helpful would it be to think about spending your money in ways that are creative, redemptive, and sustaining? A score of 1 means not helpful and 5 means very helpful to think about spending your money in terms of things that are creative, redemptive, and sustaining.

Self-identified Christians, 2020

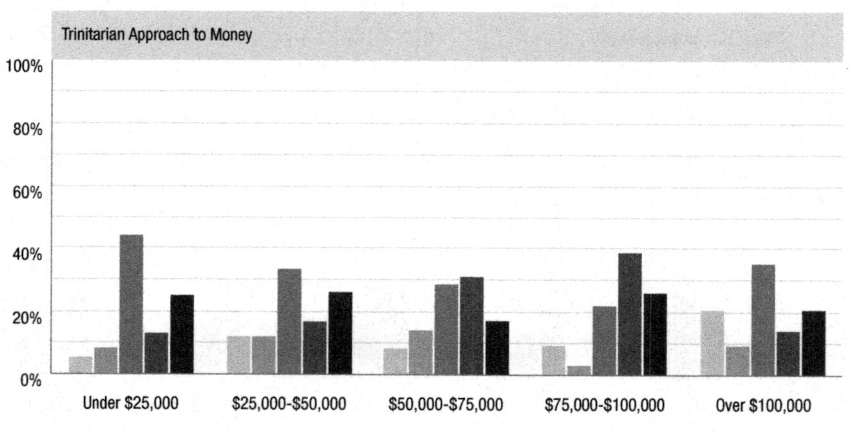

N=211; Source: Self-identified Christians in Survey Monkey Survey, July 2020

Trinitarian Approach to Money	1	2	3	4	5	TOTAL	WEIGHTED AVERAGE
Under $25,000	5.71% 2	8.57% 3	45.71% 16	14.29% 5	25.71% 9	16.59% 35	3.46
$25,000-$50,000	11.94% 8	11.94% 8	34.33% 23	16.42% 11	25.37% 17	31.75% 67	3.31
$50,000-$75,000	8.57% 3	14.29% 5	28.57% 10	31.43% 11	17.14% 6	16.59% 35	3.34
$75,000-$100,000	9.68% 3	3.23% 1	22.58% 7	38.71% 12	25.81% 8	14.69% 31	3.68
Over $100,000	20.93% 9	9.30% 4	34.88% 15	13.95% 6	20.93% 9	20.38% 43	3.05

N=211; Source: Self-identified Christians in Survey Monkey Survey, July 2020

Are there Bible stories or teachings of Jesus that affect your daily decisions about how you spend your money?

St. Francis's parishioners, 2020

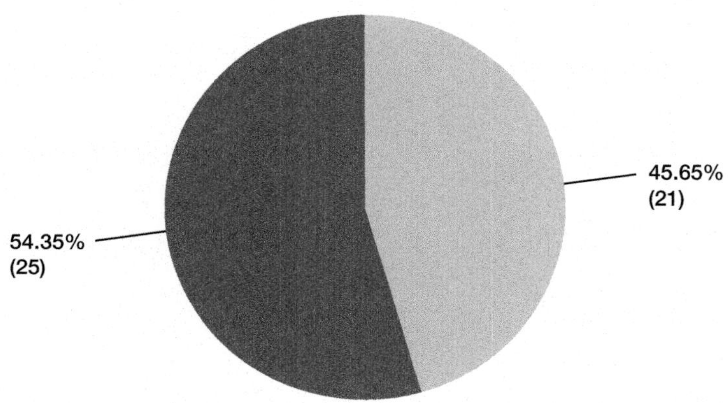

N=46; Source: St. Francis Theology & Money Survey, July 2020

NO YES

Self-identified Christians, 2020

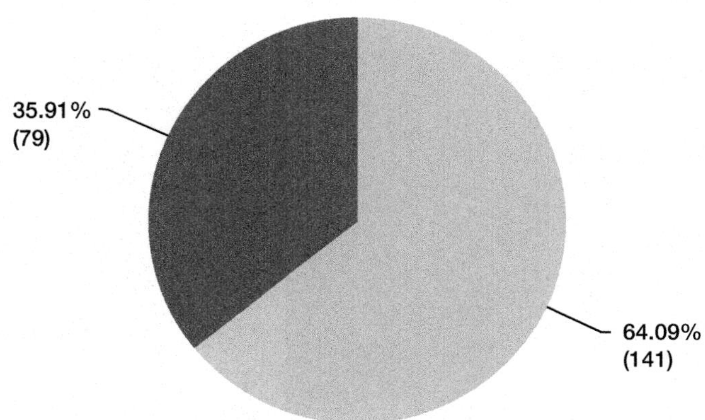

N=220; Source: Self-identified Christians in Survey Monkey Survey, July 2020

NO YES

Bibliography

Allen, Pauline. "Challenges in Approaching Patristic Texts from the Perspective of Contemporary Catholic Social Teaching." In *Reading Patristic Texts on Social Ethics*, edited by Johan Leemans, Brian J. Matz, and Johan Verstraeten, 30–42. Washington, DC: Catholic University of America Press, 2011.

Althaus-Reid, Marcella. *Indecent Theology: Theological Perversions in Sex, Gender, and Politics.* London: Routledge, 2000.

"The American Gay Rights Movement," ThoughtCo. February 7, 2019. *https://www.thoughtco.com/american-gay-rights-movement-721309.*

"Asian Americans: Diverse and Growing." *Population Bulletin* 53, no. 2: 1–40.

Bassler, Jouette M. "1 Corinthians." In *Women's Biblical Commentary*, 20th anniversary ed., edited by Carol A. Newsom, Sharon H. Ringe, and Jacqueline E. Lapsley, 557–565. Louisville, KY: Westminster John Knox Press, 2012.

Bieringer, Reimund. "Texts That Create a Future." In *Reading Patristic Texts on Social Ethics*, edited by Johan Leemans, Brian J. Matz, and Johan Verstraeten, 3–29. Washington, DC: Catholic University of America Press, 2011.

Bleiweis, Robin. "Quick Facts about the Gender Wage Gap." Center for American Progress. March 24, 2020. *https://www.americanprogress.org/issues/women/reports/2020/03/24/482141/quick-acts-gender-wage-gap/.*

Boff, Leonardo, and Clodovis Boff. *Introduction to Liberation Theology.* Translated by Paul Burns. Maryknoll, NY: Orbis, 2016.

Book of Common Prayer. New York: Church Publishing, 2007.

Bosch, Adriana, series producer. *Latino Americans.* Episode 1, "Foreigners in Their Own Land." Aired September 2013, on PBS. *https://www.pbs.org/show/latino-americans/.*

Brothers, Greg. "Patrons and Patronage in the Early Christian Church." *Ministry: International Journal of Pastors.* July 2002. *https://www.ministrymagazine.org/archive/2002/07/patrons-and-patronage-in-the-early-christian-church.html.*

Brown, Brené. *The Gifts of Imperfection: Let Go of Who You Think You're Supposed to Be and Embrace Who You Are.* Center City, MN: Hazelden Publishing, 2010.

Brown, Eric. "Aristotle on the Choice of Lives: Two Concepts of Self-Sufficiency." Accessed October 5, 2021. *https://philpapers.org/rec/BROAOT-2.*

Brown, Peter. *Through the Eye of a Needle: Wealth, the Fall of Rome, and the Making of Christianity in the West, 350–550 AD.* Princeton, NJ: Princeton University Press, 2012.

Brueggemann, Walter. *Journey to the Common Good.* Louisville, KY: Westminster John Knox Press, 2010.

———. *Money and Possessions.* Louisville, KY: Westminster John Knox Press, 2016.

Busette, Camille. "Tax Reform in the Age of Inequality." The Brookings Institute, October 2, 2017. *https://www.brookings.edu/blog/fixgov/2017/10/02/tax-reform-in-the-age-of-inequality/.*

Cavanaugh, William T. *Being Consumed: Economics and Christian Desire.* Grand Rapids, MI: Eerdmans, 2008.

Christoffersen, John. "Rising Inequality 'Most Important Problem,' Says Nobel-Winning Economist." *St. Louis Post-Dispatch.* October 14, 2013.

D'Andrea, Laura Tyson, and Ceri Parker. "An Economist Explains Why Women Are Paid Less." World Economic Forum. March 9, 2019. *https://www.weforum.org/agenda/2019/03/an-economist-explains-why-women-get-paid-less/.*

De La Torre, Miguel A. *Reading the Bible from the Margins.* Maryknoll, NY: Orbis Books, 2002.

de Leeuw, Gawain. *The Body of Christ in a Market Economy: An Anglican Inquiry into Economic Thinking.* New York: Peter Lang, 2019.

Discrimination in America: Experiences and Views of LGBTQ Americans. National Public Radio, Robert Wood Johnson Foundation, Harvard University T.H. Chan School of Public Health. November 2017. *https://cdn1.sph.harvard.edu/wp-content/uploads/sites/94/2017/11/NPR-RWJF-HSPH-Discrimination-LGBTQ-Final-Report.pdf.*

Dropkin, Murray, Jim Halpin, and Bill La Touche. *The Budget-Building Book for Nonprofits: A Step-by-Step Guide for Managers and Boards.* San Francisco: John Wiley & Sons, 2007.

Dussel, Enrique. *Beyond Philosophy: Ethics, History, Marxism, and Liberation Theology.* Edited by Eduardo Medieta. Lanham, MD: Rowman & Littlefield, 2003.

Ellacuría, Ignacio. *Ignacio Ellacuría: Essays on History, Liberation, and Salvation.* Edited by Michael Lee. Maryknoll, NY: Orbis Press, 2013.

Ellul, Jacques. *Money and Power.* Downers Grove, IL: InterVarsity Press, 1984.

The Episcopal Church. "The Five Marks of Mission." June 6, 2012. *http://www.episcopalchurch.org/page/five-marks-mission.*

Facundo, Alvaredo. "Inequality Over the Past Century." International Monetary Fund. September 2011. *https://www.imf.org/external/pubs/ft/fandd/2011/09/picture.htm.*

Fahmy, Dalia. "European Countries That Have Mandatory Church Taxes Are about as Religious as Their Neighbors That Don't." Pew Research Center. May 9, 2019. *https://www.pewresearch.org/fact-tank/2019/05/09/european-countries-that-have-mandatory-church-taxes-are-about-as-religious-as-their-neighbors-that-dont/.*

Faltas, Iberkis. "Gender Wage Inequality: Still a Long Way to Go." *PA Times.* July 27, 2018. *https://patimes.org/gender-wage-inequality-still-a-long-way-to-go/.*

Firer Hinze, Christine. "What Is Enough? Catholic Social Thought, Consumption, and Material Sufficiency." In *Having: Property and*

Possession in Religious and Social Life, edited by William Schweiker and Charles Matthews, 162–188. Grand Rapids, MI: Eerdmans, 2004.

Foster, Richard J. *Celebration of Discipline: The Path to Spiritual Growth.* Special anniversary ed. New York: HarperOne, 2018.

Friedman, Edwin H. *A Failure of Nerve.* 10th anniversary rev. ed. Edited by Margaret M. Treadwell and Edward W. Beal. New York: Church Publishing, 2017.

Gebara, Ivone. *Longing for Running Water: Ecofeminism and Liberation.* Minneapolis: Fortress Press, 1999.

Girard, René. *Things Hidden Since the Foundation of the World.* Translated by Stephen Bann and Michael Metteer. Stanford, CA: Stanford University Press, 1978.

Gonzales, Christian, Sonali Jain-Chandra, Kalpana Kochlar, Monique Newiak, and Tlek Zeinullayev. "Catalyst for Change: Empowering Women and Tackling Income Inequality." IMF Staff Discussion Note. October 2015. *https://www.imf.org/external/pubs/ft/sdn/2015/sdn1520.pdf.*

González, Justo L. *Faith and Wealth: A History of Early Christian Ideas on the Origin, Significance, and Use of Money.* Eugene, OR: Wipf and Stock Publishers, 2002.

Goodchild, Philip. *Theology of Money.* Durham, NC: Duke University Press, 2009.

Gruberg, Sharita, Lindsay Mahowald, and John Halpin. "The State of the LGBTQ Community in 2020." Center for American Progress. October 6, 2020. *https://www.americanprogress.org/issues/lgbtq-rights/reports/2020/10/06/491052/state-lgbtq-community-2020/.*

Gutiérrez, Gustavo. *A Theology of Liberation.* Rev. ed. Edited and translated by Sister Caridad Inda and John Eagleson. Maryknoll, NY: Orbis Press, 2014.

Harlan, Beckley. "Theology and Prudence in John Ryan's Economic Ethics." In *Religion and Public Life: The Legacy of Monsignor John A. Ryan*, edited by Robert G. Kennedy, Mary Christine Athans, Bernard

V. Brady, William C. McDonough, and Michael J. Naughton, 5–10. Lanham, MD: University Press of America, 2001.

Heifetz, Ronald, and Marty Linsky. *Leadership on the Line: Staying Alive through the Dangers of Change*. Boston: Harvard Business Review Press, 2017.

Hicks, Douglas A. *Inequality and Christian Ethics*. Cambridge: Cambridge University Press, 2000.

Institute for Policy Studies. "Fact: Gender Economic Inequality." Accessed November 7, 2020. *https://inequality.org/facts/gender-inequality/*.

———. "Fact: Racial Economic Inequality." Accessed November 3, 2020. *https://inequality.org/facts/racial-inequality/*.

———. "Values and Skills for Purpose." September 21, 2010. Trinity Cathedral, Phoenix, AZ. *https://day1.org/articles/5d9b820ef71918cd-f2002b8f/the_most_rev_katharine_jefferts_schori_values_and_skills_for_a_purpose*.

Johnson, Elizabeth. "Ephesians." In *Women's Biblical Commentary*, 20th anniversary ed. Edited by Carol A. Newsom, Sharon H. Ringe, and Jacqueline E. Lapsley, 576–580. Louisville, KY: Westminster John Knox Press, 2012.

Johnson, Luke Timothy. *Sharing Possessions: What Faith Demands*, 2nd ed. Grand Rapids, MI: Eerdmans, 2011.

Johnson Lewis, Jone. "A Short History of Women's Property Rights in the United States." ThoughtCo. July 13, 2019. *https://www.thoughtco.com/property-rights-of-women-3529578*.

Keucher, Gerald W. *Remember the Future: Financial Leadership and Asset Management for Congregations*. New York: Church Publishing, 2006.

"Key Dates in U.S. Military LGBT Policy." Naval History Blog, U.S. Naval Institute. March 26, 2018. *https://www.navalhistory.org/2018/03/26/key-dates-in-u-s-military-lgbt-policy*.

Kocher, Sarah. "Nearly Half of Women Face Gender Discrimination Almost Every Day." *New York Post*. March 2, 2020. *https://nypost.com/2020/03/02/nearly-half-of-women-face-gender-discrimination-almost-every-day/*.

Krueger, David A. "Can John Ryan's Economic Ethic Work for a Global Economy?" In *Religion and Public Life: The Legacy of Monsignor John A. Ryan*, edited by Robert G. Kennedy, Mary Christine Athans, Bernard V. Brady, William C. McDonough, and Michael J. Naughton, 197–210. Lanham, MD: University Press of America, 2001.

Lansdell, Henry. *The Sacred Tenth or Studies in Tithe-Giving Ancient and Modern*. Grand Rapids: Baker, 1954.

Leemans, Johan, and John Verstraeten. "The (Im)possible Dialogue between Patristic and Catholic Social Thought." In *Reading Patristic Texts on Social Ethics*, edited by Johan Leemans, Brian J. Matz, and Johan Verstraeten, 222–31. Washington, DC: Catholic University of America Press, 2011.

Leonhardt, Megan. "75% of Millennial Couples Talk about Money at Least Once a Week—and It Seems to Be Working for Them." CNBC.com. July 31, 2018. *https://www.cnbc.com/2018/07/27/75-percent-of-millennial-couples-talk-about-money-at-least-once-a-week.html.*

Levinson, Kate. *Emotional Currency: A Woman's Guide to Building a Healthy Relationship with Money*. Berkeley, CA: Celestial Arts, 2011.

Long, Stephen D. *Divine Economy: Theology and the Market*. New York: Routledge, 2000.

Lui, Meizhu, Barbara Robles, Betsy Leondar-Wright, Rose Brewer, and Rebecca Adamson, with United for a Fair Economy. *The Color of Wealth: The Story Behind the U.S. Racial Wealth Divide*. New York: The New Press, 2006.

Lutz, David W. "Christian Social Thought and Corporate Governance." In *Religion and Public Life: The Legacy of Monsignor John A. Ryan*, edited by Robert G. Kennedy, Mary Christine Athans, Bernard V. Brady, William C. McDonough, and Michael J. Naughton, 121–40. Lanham, MD: University Press of America, 2001.

MacCulloch, Diarmaid. *Christianity: The First Three Thousand Years*. New York: Penguin, 2010.

Marcuson, Margaret J. *Leaders Who Last: Sustaining Yourself and Your Ministry*. New York: Seabury Books, 2009.

———. *Money and Your Ministry*. Portland, OR: Marcuson Leadership Circle, 2014.

Martin, Emily. "Shortchanging Women: Four Reasons Why It Takes Women 10 Years to Earn a Man's Pay." *U.S. News and World Report*. April 4, 2017. *https://www.usnews.com/opinion/civil-wars/articles/2017-04-04/on-equal-pay-day-4-reasons-women-make-less-money-than-men*.

Masci, David. "Key Facts about Government-Funded Religion around the World." Pew Research Center. October 3, 2017. *https://www.pewresearch.org/fact-tank/2017/10/03/key-facts-about-government-favored-religion-around-the-world/*.

Matz, Brian. "The Principle of Detachment from Private Property in Basil of Caesarea's Homily 6 and Its Content." In *Reading Patristic Texts on Social Ethics*, edited by Johan Leemans, Brian J. Matz, and Johan Verstraeten., 161–84. Washington, DC: Catholic University of America Press, 2011.

McCarraher, Eugene. *The Enchantment of Mammon: How Capitalism Became the Religion of Modernity*. Cambridge, MA: The Belknap Press of Harvard University Press, 2019.

McKenna, Kevin E. *A Concise Guide to Catholic Social Teaching*. 3rd ed. Notre Dame, IN: Ave Maria Press, 2019.

Miller, Susan. "'Shocking' Numbers: Half of LGBTQ Adults Live in States Where No Laws Ban Job Discrimination." *USA Today*. October 8, 2019. *https://www.usatoday.com/story/news/nation/2019/10/08/lgbt-employment-discrimination-half-of-states-offer-no-protections/3837244002/*.

Mobley, Gregory. "What the Rabbi Taught the Reverend about the Baby Jesus." In *My Neighbor's Faith: Stories of Interreligious Encounter, Growth, and Transformation*, edited by Jennifer Howe Peace, Or N. Rose, and Gregory Mobley, 48–50. Maryknoll, NY: Orbis Books, 2012.

Morgan, Dan. "Hate Crimes Against Asian and Black People Rise Sharply in U.S., FBI Says." CNBC. August 30, 2021. *https://www.cnbc.com/2021/08/30/fbi-says-hate-crimes-against-asian-and-black-people-rise-in-the-us.html*.

Murray, Julio E. "The AGAPE Economy: The Church's Call to Action." *The Anglican Theological Review* 98, no 1. (Winter 2016): 122–36.

Murphy, James W, ed. *Faithful Investing: The Power of Decisive Action and Incremental Change*. New York: Church Publishing, 2019.

Niebuhr, H. Richard, "The Religion of Christianity and Democracy." In *Theology, History, and Culture: Major Unpublished Works of H. Richard Niebuhr*, edited by William Stacey Johnson. New Haven, CT: Yale University Press, 1996.

Noll, Mark A. *The Old Religion in a New World: The History of North American Christianity*. Grand Rapids, MI: Eerdmans, 2002.

Notte, Jason. "Why Millennials Aren't Afraid to Talk about Money." TheStreet.com. November 8, 2017. *https://www.thestreet.com/story/14355305/1/why-millennials-talk-about-money.html.*

Novak, Michael. *The Spirit of Democratic Capitalism*. Lanham, MD: Madison Books, 1982.

O'Brien Steinfels, Margaret. "The Contemporary Importance of Monsignor John A. Ryan and Catholic Social Thought." In *Religion and Public Life: The Legacy of Monsignor John A. Ryan*, edited by Robert G. Kennedy, Mary Christine Athans, Bernard V. Brady, William C. McDonough, and Michael J. Naughton, 291–98. Lanham, MD: University Press of America, 2001.

Oliver, Melvin L., and Thomas M. Shapiro. *Black Wealth/White Wealth: A New Perspective on Racial Inequality*. 10th anniversary ed. New York: Routledge, 1995.

Packer, Michael. "Jesus Talked the Most about . . . Money?" Smyrna Patch. July 23, 2011. *http://patch.com/georgia/smyrna/jesus-talked-the-most-aboutmoney.*

Painter, George. "The Sensibilities of Our Forefathers: The History of Sodomy Laws in the United States." Sodomy Laws. January 31, 2005. *http://www.glapn.org/sodomylaws/sensibilities/districtofcolumbia.htm.*

Palmer, Parker. *Healing the Heart of Democracy: The Courage to Create a Politics Worthy of the Human Spirit.* San Francisco: Jossey-Bass, 2011.

Patterson, Jane, and Steven Tomlinson. "A Framework for Rule-Crafting Practice." Austin, TX: Seminary of the Southwest, 2018.

Pawlikowski, John T. "Papal Teaching on Economic Justice: Change and Continuity." In *Religion and Public Life: The Legacy of Monsignor John A. Ryan*, edited by Robert G. Kennedy, Mary Christine Athans, Bernard V. Brady, William C. McDonough, and Michael J. Naughton, 75–94. Lanham, MD: University Press of America, 2001.

Petrella, Ivan. *Beyond Liberation Theology: A Polemic*. London: SCM Press, 2008.

Poole, Eve. *Buying God: Consumerism and Theology*. New York: Church Publishing Incorporated, 2019.

———. *Capitalism's Toxic Assumptions: Redefining Next Generation Economics*. London: Bloomsbury, 2015.

Pope John Paul II. "Working as a Sharing in the Activity of the Creation," in *Laborem Exercens* (Through Work). September 14, 1981. *http://www.vatican.va/content/john-paul-ii/en/encyclicals/documents/hf_jp-ii_enc_14091981_laborem-exercens.html.*

Prentiss, Demi. *Making Money Holy*. New York: Church Publishing, 2020.

Prichard, Robert W. *A History of the Episcopal Church*. New York: Morehouse Publishing, 2014.

"Prosperity Gospel." *Christianity Today*. Accessed November 4, 2017. *https://www.christianitytoday.com/ct/topics/p/prosperity-gospel/.*

Reumann, John H. *Stewardship and the Economy of God*. Eugene, OR: Wipf and Stock, 1992.

Rhee, Helen. "Wealth, Poverty, and Eschatology." In *Reading Patristic Texts on Social Ethics*, edited by Johan Leemans, Brian J. Matz, and Johan Verstraeten, 64–84. Washington, DC: Catholic University of America Press, 2011.

Rieger, Jorge. *No Rising Tide: Theology, Economics, and the Future*. Minneapolis: Fortress Press, 2009.

Salstrand, George A. *The Story of Stewardship in the United States of America*. Grand Rapids, MI: Baker, 1956.

Salvatierra, Alexia, and Peter Heltzel. *Faith-Rooted Community Organizing: Mobilizing the Church in Service to the World.* Downers Grove, IL: IVP Books, 2014.

Schnelle, Udo. *Theology of the New Testament.* Translated by M. Eugene Boring. Grand Rapids, MI: Baker Academic, 2009.

Schor, Juliet B. *Plentitude: The New Economics of True Wealth.* New York: Penguin Press, 2010.

Schori, Katharine Jefferts. "Presiding Bishop's Sermon at Christ Church Cathedral, Nashville." Episcopaldigitalnetwork.com. September 22, 2013. *http://episcopaldigitalnetwork.com/ens/2013/09/22/presiding-bishops-sermon-at-christ-church-cathedral-nashville.*

Schut, Michael. ed. *Money and Faith: The Search for Enough.* New York: Morehouse Publishing, 2008.

"Selected Population Profile in the United States." United States Census Bureau. Archived from the original on February 12, 2020. *https://data.census.gov.*

Simmons, Luke. "Why Doesn't the Apostle Paul Speak Against Slavery?" Redemption Gateway. September 21, 2018. *https://gateway.redemptionaz.com/why-doesnt-the-apostle-paul-speak-against-slavery/.*

Simonsen, Mario Henrique. *Brasil 2002.* 6th ed. Rio de Janeiro: APEC, 1976.

Singh, Devin. *Divine Currency: The Theological Power of Money in the West.* Stanford, CA: Stanford University Press, 2018.

Sitze, Bob. *Stewardshift: An Economia for Congregational Change.* New York: Church Publishing, 2016.

Skidelsky, Robert, and Edward Skidelsky. *How Much Is Enough? Money and the Good Life.* New York: Other Press, 2012.

Steinke, Peter L. *Congregational Leadership in Anxious Times.* Lanham, MD: Rowman & Littlefield, 2006.

Sung, Jung Mo. *Desire, Market, Religion.* London: SCM Press, 2007.

Tanner, Kathryn. *Christianity and the New Spirit of Capitalism.* New Haven, CT: Yale University Press, 2019.

———. *Economy of Grace.* Minneapolis: Fortress Press, 2005.

———. *Jesus, Humanity, and the Trinity: A Brief Systematic Theology*. Minneapolis: Fortress Press, 2001.

Thornton, James. *Wealth and Poverty in the Teachings of the Church Fathers*. Manchester, MO: St. John Chrysostom Press, 1993.

Traflet, Janice, and Robert E. Wright. "America Doesn't Just Have a Gender Pay Gap. It Has a Gender Wealth Gap." *Washington Post*. April 2, 2019. *https://www.washingtonpost.com/outlook/2019/04/02/america-doesnt-just-have-gender-pay-gap-it-has-gender-wealth-gap/*.

United Nations. "Millennium Goals." Accessed December 4, 2016. *http://www.un.org/millenniumgoals/*.

———. "Sustainable Development Goals." Accessed December 4, 2016. *http://www.un.org/sustainabledevelopment/sustainable-development-goals*.

Van Nuffelen, Peter. "Social Ethics and Moral Discourse in Late Antiquity." In *Reading Patristic Texts on Social Ethics*, edited by Johan Leemans, Brian J. Matz, and Johan Verstraeten, 45–63. Washington, DC: Catholic University of America Press, 2011.

Wallis, Jim. *Rediscovering Values: A Guide for Economic and Moral Recovery*. New York: Howard Books, 2011.

Ward, Marguerite. "The Most Dangerous Jobs for Men." CNBC. January 4, 2017. *https://www.cnbc.com/2017/01/04/the-10-most-dangerous-jobs-for-men.html*.

Wariboko, Nimi. *God and Money: A Theology of Money in a Globalizing World*. Lanham, MD: Lexington Books, 2008.

Waters, Brent. *Just Capitalism: A Christian Ethic of Economic Globalization*. Louisville, KY: Westminster John Knox Press, 2016.

Welby, Justin. *Dethroning Mammon: Making Money Serve Grace*. London: Bloomsbury, 2016.

Wheeler, Sondra Ely. *Wealth as Peril and Obligation: The New Testament on Possession*. Grand Rapids, MI: Eerdmans, 1995.

"Why Was the Church So Powerful in the Middle Ages." Reference. April 5, 2020. *https://www.reference.com/history/church-powerful-middle-ages-61234fd15059a12d*.

Wilder, Barbara. *Money Is Love: Reconnecting to the Sacred Origins of Money.* Santa Fe, NM: Wild Ox Press, 2010.

Williams, Rowan, and Larry Elliott. *Crisis and Recovery, Ethics, Economics, and Justice*. Houndmills, UK: Palgrave Macmillan, 2010.

Woodley, Randy S. *Shalom and the Community of Creation: An Indigenous Vision.* Grand Rapids, MI: Eerdmans, 2012.

World Bank. "Poverty: Overview." October 7, 2020. *https://www.worldbank.org/en/topic/poverty/overview*.

Young, Francis M., and David F. Ford. *Meaning and Truth in Second Corinthians*. Eugene, OR: Wipf and Stock, 1987.

Zabriskie, Marek P., ed. *The Social Justice Bible Challenge: A 40 Day Bible Challenge*. Cincinnati, OH: Forward Movement, 2017.